This volume is distributed free of charge so that everyone may know the messages of the Most Holy Mary,
Queen of Peace. May we remind you therefore that no
one is authorized to ask for sums of money, contribu-
tions or offerings for the book; it is a gesture of faith
in the messages. *(Mt. 6, 24-34)*.
We ask those who wish to repay us, to pray especially
for the most distant souls.

PRAY WITH YOUR HEART

Meditations of Fr. Tomislav Vlašić and Fr. Slavko Barbarić
from July to December 1985

MILAN 1986

The books: * OPEN YOUR HEARTS TO MARY QUEEN OF PEACE
          * ABANDON YOURSELVES TOTALLY TO ME
          * PRAY WITH YOUR HEART

are available from:

IRELAND:
GERALD LODGE
31 Pinewood Park - Rathfarnham, Dublin 14 - Tel. 932883

SCOTLAND:
CRAIG LODGE
Dalmally, Argylishire, PA33 1AR - Scotland - Tel. (083 82) 216

ENGLAND & WALES:
JOHN MAC MAHON
70 Merrivale Road - Rising Brook - Stafford ST 17 9EE - Tel. (0785) 47897

CANADA: Sr. DANIELA A. ORAZZO
St. Theresa's Day Care Centre Carmelite Missionary Sisters
1196 Wilson Ave - Downsview, Ont. M3M 1H3
Tel. (416) 6366123 - 6381560

U.S.A.:
TERESA MANAX
407 West Oak Street - 76691 West - Texas - Tel. (817) 826.3721
MARY QUEEN OF PEACE CENTER
P.O. Box 527, West, Texas 76691, Tel. (817) 826-4244

SINGAPORE:
Miss JACQUELINE WEBB
« SHALOM »
151A King's Road
11-04 Singapore 1926
Republic of Singapore - Tel. 4744240

AUSTRALIA:
LEON LEGRAND
P.O. Box 523
Mt. Eliza, Vic. 3930 - (03) 787 4539

TO MARY QUEEN OF PEACE
with love from her children
of the Milan and Lecco groups

*« The moment of prayer is the moment of the
transfiguration of the soul, we must therefore be prepared
to put everything on the Cross, since only if the old self dies
shall we be transformed. We must allow Jesus to operate
this transformation, this transfiguration of our souls.
There, my wish is that you may follow these messages,
mostly by means of a continuous, daily, silent and deep
prayer in order to be transformed.
And it would be nice, very nice indeed, if people were to
say of you: "The best thing I saw today were the eyes
of that man I met in the street". If we were thus to be
witnesses before people, soon the world would be changed.
transfigured. Try and do it, so as to be witnesses of the
transfiguration of Jesus in your hearts ».*

(Fr. Tomislav Vlašić, 6 August 1985)

Milan, 10 March 1986

On publishing in Italian the fourth volume « I beseech you to listen to my messages and live them » we inserted the following invitation.

Dear Friends in the Heart of Mary Queen of Peace,

This is an invitation to spread the messages given in Medjugorje, according to that which Our Lady has said several times, « *Your task is to accept Divine peace, to live it and to spread it* ».

The Association of Friends of Medjugorje, which has taken up and practised this invitation over the past two years, now intends to extend this initiative to those who, like us, feel the necessity of adhering to Our Lady's request, giving to others without asking for anything in return.

We believe that the first monthly message (25th January, 1987) could bring us to this understanding:

« *Dear children. Now I want to invite every one of you to begin from today to live the new life. Dear children, I want you to understand that God has chosen each one of you as instruments in the plan for the salvation of mankind. You cannot understand how great your role is in God's plan. Therefore, dear children, pray so that in prayer you may understand God's plan through you. I am with you so that you may accomplish it fully* ».

Our reply to those desirous to help spread the messages is to join the associations which have already been formed for the purpose of spreading, free of charge, the messages (U.S.A. - Ireland - England and Wales - Scotland), or to form new ones in your own countries.

Our Lady's request to offer ourselves as a sacrifice for other finds a means of real fulfilment here.

I greet you in the sign of peace and love.

MARIO BRUGHERA
for the Association

INDEX

INTRODUCTION

Our Lady Queen of Peace is continuing to guide the Medjugorje parish.

Through the meditations of Fr. Tomislav Vlašić and Fr. Slavko Barbarić we offer you the outline of the spiritual path of the second six-month period of 1985.

As in the previous publications, the readers will also be able to find some brief items of news on the development of events, as recounted by the Fathers.

The texts have been transcribed from tape recordings, omitting only those parts which were merely repetitions of news or messages. After the meditations we have listed those messages Our Lady has given to the parish of Medjugorje every Thursday or on particular anniversaries or solemnities, from the beginning (1 March 1984) up to and including December 1985.

Alberto Bonifacio - Mario Brughera

There may be some inaccuracies due both to the fact that the Yugoslav Fathers found some difficulty in expressing themselves in Italian, and that they were unable to correct the proofs.

The editors therefore assume full responsibility for the transcriptions and in every case they can guarantee the authenticity of the texts.

MEDITATIONS
OF FR. TOMISLAV VLAŠIĆ AND FR. SLAVKO BARBARIĆ

« Pray, fast, have faith »

With regard to the latest events in Medjugorje – there are events in Medjugorje and there are events in the press. When one talks of Medjugorje regarding press articles which are critical of it, the path to follow is the one indicated in the 1st reading of the Feast of St. Peter: « St. Peter, watched by two guards and tied with two chains, was sleeping, whilst just outside the iron gate the sentries were guarding the gaol... ».
At this point something happens: « Wake up, arise, get dressed! » and an angel leads him through the gate into the street.
What strikes me here is the presence of the Father who takes care of his children, even when everything appears impossible. St. Peter is asleep in chains and the opposing forces are on guard, ready; on the human level it is impossible to save him, whilst on the divine one everything is possible, everything begins to move and he is saved. God wakes people up and takes the steps that a mother and father usually take towards their child. « Wake up – he says – get up, get dressed and walk ». And when he is well on his way, he says, « Now you are capable of walking on your own – go! ».
What happened, in my opinion, has happened for two reasons: one, because the Church has not brandished the sword against Herod, but has, instead, got down to praying unceasingly, and two, because St. Peter has put himself totally at God's disposal by being ready to be crucified.
St. Paul says, « Everybody has abandoned me, but the Lord has been near to me and has given me strength ».
The same applies to Medjugorje and to whomever wants to walk

in God's path. Medjugorje is often on trial, but never in crisis, because a crisis is something interior, whereas trials are exterior. Everyone who wants to move forward in one's faith will be tried; the more forward one is, the more one is tried. He who wants to climb a higher mountain will have to surmount bigger obstacles, and the same goes for faith.

For me, Medjugorje is a divine grace for the whole world and, therefore, we must not wonder whether we are being and will be tried; however, on looking back at it from the beginning, we have been undergoing trials during all the time of the apparitions and in no trial were we strong enough to face it.

It is God who has taken care of everything; we were not capable of overcoming our trials, but God has seen to it all.

I can say at this moment that God guides everything and that there will be still harder trials, since salvation has to go right down to its roots. We cannot be healed by theories, but we are healed, we are saved through God's work – the kind of love which, embodied in the church, for all those who want to follow Christ radically goes as far as sacrificing one's life for God, suffering for Him and offering one's own blood for Him.

This is the maximum Jesus accomplished for us and, if we want to belong to God until the end, then we must cross the path on which God's salvation is fulfilled.

When we talk of conversion, we cannot debate it on a theoretical level, but we must practise it in such a way that our old self is truly destroyed. It follows that we can also expect the destruction of a false world around us. In the Gospel we have, therefore, two choices: – the first one telling us, « Be converted, so that you may not be destroyed », and the second one, « If you will not be converted you shall all perish together ».

When I am talking about conversion, we must understand that it is not something theoretical. And so, I make a plan and move slowly slowly; above all, allowing God to guide me along various ways and to even make me suffer, to even make me destroy the false world within me, including the false world, as it were, within the Church herself and all of us. If we are able to face all this, then we can honestly expect some results. The same could be said of a house we intend to renovate; we have to pull down walls, get rid of so many things, sometimes we even have to sleep outside, in order to put everything right, so that everything might be renewed. We are incapable of seeing all these things by ourselves alone. God, on the other hand, sees even the falseness within us and the world. We have to allow God to lead us through these trials. I am telling you – try not to fall into a crisis; that is why I would like to stress the fact that the primitive church used to pray whilst its leaders were on trial. She used to pray, without discussing. She did not fear, nor did she write any articles on the subject, or worry, but prayed, abandoning herself to the Lord.

It is God who is then able to guide those in authority, events, no matter how chained up everything might look, because everything is possible to God – starting from the Virgin's womb, where the impossible human logic began, the one that we ourselves, as well, must follow in the same way the Saints Peter and Paul did.

It is useless looking just at the messages given by Our Lady, as there are many pilgrims who learn the messages by heart – I repeat it is useless! The pharisees also knew the scriptures by heart.

Our Lady is, for us, a sign; he, however, who despite having understood the sign does not go ahead shows himself not to have understood the sign in the first place, since the sign is there not for its own sake, but in order to enable us to move forward. Our Lady, therefore, does not answer questions, She does not give out recipes, but simply says, « *Pray, fast and have faith* ». And this means going beyond the sign. Open yourselves to the Holy Spirit, may He enlighten you to understand the times, your sickness, your difficulties. And so, even in moments of trial, as now, all of you pilgrims must lead the others to a positive attitude of hope. The attitude of Medjugorje is the attitude of peace, which is the root of hope, and the fruit of hope is peace.

You must not, therefore, in the moments of trial lose your head and allow yourselves to become prey to anxieties, to fears. Our Lady said, « *These come from satan* ». We must, instead, be full of peace, using the very weapons Our Lady pointed out to us

13

– prayer, fasting, fraternal love and humility – with these alone will we overcome all obstacles and be stronger in all adversities. This is all very important for priests, for group leaders – that they should bring this hope. Trials are themselves a grace, since only when on trial and after undergoing one, can we see and understand more clearly, better, and can go further ahead. Without trials one cannot go further, one cannot deepen one's faith. Look, therefore, at your trials with peace, with joy, carrying on praying, loving, offering everything to God.

The messages given by Our Lady become slowly, slowly, for us, similar one to the other. For those who accept them with an open heart all messages are similar because they encourage us, call us again and enlighten us; but this applies only to those who go forward.

To those who have sat down and stay put, no new message whatsoever can bring light, but instead it will only disturb them. It disturbs them, as the message wants people to walk, whereas people want to stay put and say, « we are disturbed by this logic, by these messages ».

What I want to tell you is – be brave, go ahead, do not worry! If someone puts the messages in doubt, do not allow that to happen. If a Christian doubts about peace, love, penance, prayer, then we have been throwing our words to the pigs.

We have thrown out of the church even our own saints, and yet they have become saints thanks to the fact that they have been following this path. So, there is not much to discuss with people on what might be the extraordinary happenings of Medjugorje, but rather there is a great deal to talk about on a fundamental, spiritual level and to tell people, « If you believe, this is the way leading to God, to the Gospel ». He who does not believe takes the easy way out. I must believe.

Our Lady is inviting us to this, but as we do not want to accept this way towards God, we are disturbed by Our Lady who is telling us: « *Be converted, pray* », We need go no further than this: it is necessary to understand the fundamental points and then Our Lady's message will become clear to us.

This I wanted to tell you – get stronger, do not argue, do not talk things over much, but pray.

Trials are there so that we may become stronger and the others may grow. They will grow, though, only to the degree in which you will be the spokesman of hope, and hope always brings security, joy and peace. And what happened to Saint Peter will happen to everybody. God will lead the Church to the salvation of the world.

(Fr. Tomislav Vlašić - 1 July 1985)

« As long as you are closed, I cannot talk to you, I cannot give you graces »

Last time we heard how Jesus was sent away from his own country, how God who is omnipotent, was driven from his country and could not, therefore, perform any miracles. By this, you can see the resistance in their souls. Also to-morrow you will listen to this reading and witness how souls put up resistance. On the other hand, you will hear in the Gospel, « Go, preach, testify », and Jesus sends his apostles without any human means, any power whatsoever, but just says – « Go... ».

If you listened to the Gospel well to-day, you will have heard Jesus saying, « do not worry, but go – every hair on your head is counted, do not be afraid ».

I would like to call you to a total opening to the Lord.

Besides these six visionaries, there are two more, especially the visionary Jelena, through whom Our Lady gives messages to a prayer group on mystical life. Once when we were all gathered together and Our Lady wanted to have an evening devoted to a particular programme, a particular message, she simply said, « *I cannot talk to you, your hearts are closed...* ».

One evening two weeks ago, she told us, « *None of you has prac-tised what I told you to, therefore I cannot talk to you, I cannot give you any graces as long as you are closed...* ». That is why I am telling you, be converted. Our Lady has also invited us towards conversion, prayer, fasting and total abandonment to God. I invite you to confession and hope that each one of you may really become more of a pilgrim and that none of you may be just a tourist. Go to confession, pray, and in that way you will be able to open your hearts and be made free to receive the messages of Our Lady.

Moreover, I invite all of you to bear witness. But who can testify? Only the person who has been granted internal light and strength can.

And how can you really be sure of God's and Our Lady's presence here?

In a message through Jelena, Our Lady said, « *Each one of you has a particular personal gift and can only grasp it by himself alone, within himself* ». The light of faith is something interior, not exterior. There, indeed to-morrow you will listen to the prophet Amos, a herdsman, who says, « The Lord took me from caring for my flocks and told me, "Go and prophesy to my people, Israel" ». This is inner light. And so, you and I must be ready to welcome this inner light; and it is when there is inner light that we are able to realise the presence of Our Lady.

The facts of truth and of faith cannot simply be substantiated by adequate exterior reasoning – you must instead start from this inner light. Do you remember when the angel came to greet Our Lady and to invite her to accept the Son of God? What would have happened if Our Lady had waited for an order? She started off from an inner certainty. And do you remember when the angel appeared to St. Joseph in his sleep? What would have happened if St. Joseph had waited for an order? He, too, started off from an inner certainty, the certainty of faith. St. Francis heard an inner voice saying, « Go and renovate my Church... ». What if he had waited for an order? Nothing ever would have been done, since everybody was against that inner conviction. I say this, because we must develop the light of faith within us and be moved by the strength of the Holy Spirit. If we are not sure within our hearts, if the light of faith is not there, then we shall doubt even our name and surname. We have to be certain at least of the fact that the only way to save the world has to be the way of peace, which one obtains through conversion, through change and through prayer. I, therefore, invite you to open your hearts in order to welcome the messages of Our Lady and with the opening of your hearts, you will be granted light and inner confidence, with which you will be able to go ahead and testify. Then, when you feel this inner strength, this inner light, do not wait for outside help, since the Lord told the apostles to leave everything, not to take weapons with them, but to just set off with confidence, as he had given them power; and we must ask him to-day and to-morrow for this power, this strength and inner light, so as to be able to go forth and to announce. How can we go about announcing? Do not go into the cities, Milan, Rome, Turin and shout, « Our Lady has appeared! ». In a message to a prayer group Our Lady said, « *When you carry my messages, try not to be robbed. Carry my messages with humility, so that when people see happiness in you, they might aspire to become like you. Do not carry my message to throw it away to the others* ». This is very important; if you want to carry the message of Our Lady, start by living it and being full of divine strength, bringing happiness, salvation, one's own salvation to others.

The others will notice you are saved and will ask you, « How come you are so happy? ». And so you will start announcing, pointing out the way to salvation. There, I wish you to welcome these prophecies through the visionaries, so that you may become the people, the messengers of salvation.

Already Fr. Slavko has told you that the Rosary starts at six.

In a message, Our Lady has addressed herself to the priests asking them to pray the rosary, as the rosary will protect the Catholic Church from the evil that satan wants to bring to this era. So you priests, pray the rosary, devote time to the rosary! With this I end and give you my blessing.

(Fr. Tomislav Vlašić - 13 July 1985)

« Pray and love all men »

The four visionaries, Vicka, Marija, Ivan and Jakov are continuing with their daily apparitions. The other two have stopped having daily apparitions – Mirjana on 25 December 1982, when Our Lady promised she would appear to her on her birthday (18 March) and whenever she had any difficulties.

Our Lady has still appeared to Mirjana a few more times this year – on 18 and 19 March. Then she announced a meeting with her on 1 June and again on 12 July. Our Lady has promised to meet her again at the end of August.

Mirjana interprets these more frequent meetings by saying that she has been entrusted with announcing the first three secrets, which will be three warnings to the world and will be given before the promised sign.

The visionary is saying, « Our Lady wants everything to go ahead as planned and that I do not make any mistakes ». And, by what the visionary tells us, we can deduce that things are heading to an end.

What is remarkable is the very attitude of the visionary. When we asked her, « How do you feel to-day about being amongst young people in town? ». She told us, « If God did not give me His particular help, I would go mad ». « Why? ». She replied, « Because I know what will happen in the world and men are behaving as if God did not exist. They offend Him ».

There, in her soul, we notice a tension between what the visionary knows and the unfaithfulness of the world, of Christians themselves, who behave as if God did not exist.

With Ivanka Our Lady stopped the daily meetings on 7 May. On 6 May Ivanka received the last secret and, with this last secret,

Our Lady has concluded her account of the future of a region. This will serve as proof of the apparitions. The same evening Our Lady told her, « *Come on your own to-morrow* ».

She stayed at home all day on her own. Our Lady appeared and the encounter lasted one hour. During that encounter Our Lady gave the visionary some suggestions, reminded her of the most important moments and explained to her the secrets once again. She then asked the visionary, « *Do you have any particular wish?* ». The visionary replied, « I would like to see my mother ». Her mother had died four years ago – then her mother appeared and embraced her saying: « I am proud of you. Carry on serving God and Our Lady ». Afterwards, Our Lady asked her, « *Do you have any other wish?* ». Ivanka replied, « I would like to embrace you ». They embraced each other and Our Lady slowly moved away.

The other four visionaries carry on seeing Our Lady daily and carry her messages. Every Thursday, through Marija, Our Lady imparts a message for the parish and for all those who follow the prayers and all Our Lady is saying. *

The main theme of this month's message is the announcement of temptations. In the first message, at the beginning of the month, Our Lady exhorted the parishioners that satan might be banished from the parish and from every pilgrim. Our Lady also promised to protect everybody under her cloak. Soon after that, through Jelena, another message was announced.

The visionary saw satan in a thoughtful mood as though thinking, « Yes, I must separate some members from the prayer group. I will make others tepid, still others I will entice with several films, so that after Mass, they will rush home to watch T.V. ».

After Mass Our Lady appeared saying, « *Yes, Satan has forsaken many a place and person to come here and tempt our Medjugorje. Especially the visionaries together with the priests and prayer groups will be particular targets of temptation* ». Another message then followed through Marija, on the Thursday before last, when

---

* The text of the messages can be found on page 221.

Our Lady indicated the protection to be used against satan – She said one should have one's sacred objects blessed, one should wear them, have them in one's home as protection against satan.

Last Thursday, Our Lady said, « *I want to guide you, but you do not want to follow me* », and has invited people to accept the messages, which are God's messages through Our Lady.

So this is the main theme of this month's messages.

But there is another theme in such messages. I do not know whether you have noticed; even last year in the same period, these days were very interesting. They were full of temptations and full of graces. As you know, through Jelena and others, Our Lady told us that on 5 August 1984 her two thousandth birthday occurred and, at that time, before the actual festivity, graces were really tangible; conversions were so strong, they could not be explained. Several tourists who were heading for the seaside, felt something stopping them from doing so and found themselves going towards Medjugorje; although they had not been anywhere near to confession for a number of years, say 15, maybe 30 years, something was now changing within themselves.

Therefore, I am telling you, these are the days of grace; they will be so if we open our hearts through prayer, fasting and through total abandonment.

I have explained to you what has been happening. But now let me give you some thoughts on this and what I feel inside my heart. The sentiments I am experiencing within me at the moment are two: on the one hand I am sad, truly sad, because many responsible people of the Church do not understand Heaven's messages, because many do not set about watching, examining and looking in earnest. I am telling you – I am sad, as it is already four years now that Our Lady has been present and her presence can be photographed on the faces of the visionaries. It can be photographed, as this fact of the ecstasies is an undeniable fact, and if an event, mysterious as it may be, calls us to pray, fast, conversion, peace, and we Christians do not accept it... I cannot understand it. As far as I am concerned, it is as if someone doubted their own name. Scientific laws also exist; if we are faced with an important mystery for humanity and such a mystery explains itself, has its own explanation, we are under obligation to follow it in conscience until an explanation has been found.

So, when faced with Medjugorje's apparitions, we have to display at least this scientific, honest attitude. From the mystery lived by the visionaries, what transpires is only the call for conversion, prayer, fasting, peace and I do not know of what more a Christian should want if we accept Jesus Christ in earnest. I am sad because one does not analyse things conscientiously and does not gather the facts. These are facts and we must act accordingly; he who does not believe in the apparitions should at least believe in the call for conversion and peace. We are all aware of the fact that, if the world carries on as it is doing, it will end up in total ruin, and for this no message from Heaven is needed; all we need to do is to read the papers, listen to political debates, look at television or listen to the radio.

I really am sad as we do not accept these facts seriously, because we do not truly reflect upon the facts.

I am also sad for the many pilgrims who come here but do not abandon themselves totally to God; it seems to me, that some pilgrims come to Medjugorje, as many do, just to touch the statue of Our Lady and move on. If something happens, then fine, it happens, otherwise they go back and carry on the same path, just as before. Surely, we cannot possibly live the message of Our Lady, or of the Gospel that way.

Not one single priest in the world has ever taught us to live our Christian faith that way. We really must take faith seriously; if we do so, then we will have no trouble in understanding Our Lady. I am sad for many good pilgrims who claim that Our Lady will take care of everything by herself, if God is Almighty. This could be an illusion.

I appreciated what a father said, when presenting a German drama, where a handicapped person who had just come out of a concentration camp found that his house had been destroyed, his wife had left and he was on the street, so decided to kill himself. He threw himself into the river, but not even the river wanted him and flung him out on to the shore.

Finally, lying down facing the sky he started protesting, « God, even you have abandoned me. Where are you? ».

Then on the stage of this drama, the figure of the Heavenly Father appears saying, « Yes, I really cannot help him who, in this world, has no room left for me ».

If we do not make room for God in our lives, God cannot help us. We can stop and think of the story of salvation. God leaves us two choices, within the limits of our own freedom. He calls us, « Be converted so that you may be saved also on this earth ». If, instead, the world did not want to be converted, if Jerusalem or other towns did not want to be converted, then they would be destroyed. God carries out his plan, but such a plan can be carried out in such a way that it happens either that, « All men are saved » or that « God is right, but we are lost, we are deported in exile ».

Our conversion, our collaboration with God becomes active hope, not an illusion, not an utopia. That is why I say I am sad for so many good pilgrims who wait for something to happen for themselves, without their involvement, their fasting, their prayers, their commitment.

We must fulfill this hope the way Our Lady fulfilled it – She conceived, she accepted everything, she allowed the child to grow in her womb, she brought him into the world, she watched over him, she offered him on the cross. So, we must make this transition in life if we want to be real pilgrims who venerate Our Lady. I am really sad about these things.

On the other hand, I will tell you my joy and the path you can follow, in my opinion, so that you and the world at large may improve. I have taken as an example one of the messages imparted to Jelena by Our Lady – this is a message taken from a conversation I had with the visionary last year, 2 January 1984 – when Our Lady said, « *Pray and love all men. If you love all men, peace will also be there. If you are in peace with all men, love will also be there* ».

Our Lady always places peace and love together. For the last two weeks Our Lady has emphasised, through Jelena, the message of love several times. I felt touched by a message in particular, about a week ago, the Saturday before last when Our Lady trained us on « how to meditate on love ». First step: « *Reconcile yourselves with all men* ». And each one of us had to go through in our minds and see all the people we had conflicts with and to forgive, then in front of the group one had to recognise this need for forgiveness and ask God for his mercy. Our Lady said, « *there, if you now have open hearts all you ask of Jesus will be granted to you* ». And so, everyone prayed and, after a moment of silence, Our Lady got us to ponder on the gifts to ask God, so that our love might be complete.

Therefore, everyone had to express himself once again as to the kind of gift, so that his love might be complete.

At the end of this, we really felt well; everyone felt in a favourable disposition of soul, sensed joy and inner peace and wanted to carry on praying. But Our Lady said, « *Enough for to-night. When you have love. then you do not even need to ask Jesus, everything will be granted to you* ».

So you see – when we reach a loving attitude and when we begin to love, when our hearts overflow with love, then we do not have to even ask; this is the basis of peace. Then we do not worry anymore, since it is God who moves the world. If we are full of this love, then we are not at all worried. At the same time we are sure that God will guide everything.

Yesterday I felt particularly touched by the episode in the Gospel. In my eyes, the sign is not in the miracle of the loaves. For me, the sign, the real one, is the care of Jesus.

Nobody expected any bread from Jesus – since they did not go to a restaurant – and they certainly did not expect just that from Jesus. They went into the desert, asking, hoping to be healed, wanting to listen to some words, and I am absolutely convinced that nobody was praying in order to obtain some bread. Jesus, however, produced it, since Jesus meets our needs, since it is love that nourishes mankind. And why did all those people run after Jesus? It is believed that there were about five thousand present.

Even nowadays, with so many means of communication at our disposal, it is difficult to group five thousand people together.

So, in those days five thousand people ran after Jesus in the desert, but why? Because God loved people, went towards people, had love in him.

I remember clearly when, at the beginning of Lent, I asked Our Lady for some advice, « What must I do in the parish? ». She replied, « *Love everyone* ». I then insisted, so as to get some concrete answer, but she never gave me any. She always urged us « *to love* » and, at the end, she said, « *Look, now I am here, in every family, in every home, I am everywhere. It seems incredible, but it is possible because I love. Do the same yourselves* ».

So then I thought it over and realised that, if I love, I can influence the whole world from here. And so, if I love, and only when I love people, does everything become possible and do all the gifts begin to materialise. But you cannot really achieve this love without a great desire for God. And that is because at the core of prayer – and Our Lady underlines this – there is always a great desire for God.

Even at our last meeting on Saturday, Our Lady said, « *You tend to make mistakes, and not because you do not perform great deeds, but because you forget the small things. Because every morning you do not pray enough so as to start the day and live the way Jesus wants you to. In the evening you do not pray enough either. You do not know how to enter into prayer. You do not even make decisions, you then do not put them into action and so you become disheartened. You must react according to your needs* ».

Look at it this way – we go to eat because we feel the need to eat, we go to sleep because we feel the need to, but we only seem to go to prayer because we have been ordered to. And this is wrong, this is the wrong that destroys us. For example, we priests and nuns ought to be in prayer night and day. But if we pray according to rule, only under order, then it is the end for us. That is too little. So we ought to, right in this moment feel the need for God. I feel really good when I am with God and I can only accomplish my plans with God, in God; and so every day I take steps for the need to meet God.

For this reason I need to pray hours on end, in the same way people need to lie down on the beach, or in front of T.V. I do not have such a need, on the contrary I am well aware of the fact that it ruins me; T.V. programmes lasting two hours certainly ruin me. Instead, I need to stay at home with father, with the Heavenly Father, and really feel in his presence. This is my wish.

I told you at the beginning, that I am sad and I have given you the reason for it; I am telling you now, that I am full of hope, if we carry on doing what Our Lady does. And I beg you, in particular you who belong to various prayer movements, you who have come to Medjugorje several times – take it seriously. Do not wonder what is happening in Medjugorje. We often ask for news, but all you will ever receive for your life is in prayer itself. These days we have been having some problems here in Medjugorje, so I have asked a question through Marija, the visionary, « What must I do? ». Our Lady only pointed out the path to be followed by saying, « *I will help you understand what I want* ».

The message you bring home is very important. Our Lady and Jesus tell you, « *I will help you understand what you are supposed to do* ». What you must do, though, is to be open to the Holy Spirit, you must pray – guided by the peace and love of your souls – you will be enlightened on everything you will have to do. I beg you to make your way on the road to love. I will give you an example that will help you take your first steps. Yesterday, I read a book about an American convert who was telling his friends he had found happiness in Jesus Christ and being ridiculed for it. He eventually managed to bring a group to listen to a certain preacher, but no one listened and instead mocked him. In the end someone got up, went up to the preacher and said, « Enough of that. Get out of here. I have lived with my family in a tunnel, in absolute poverty, and I just cannot stand people with brand new shoes on ». The preacher took off his shoes, gave them to him and said, « Take them ». He got into New York bare footed; the road was wet and people turned round to look at him and said, « He is mad ». The same young man took a look at him and, as he lost sight of him behind a block, said, « For the first time I believe in Jesus Christ ».

Here we witness how love opens the road to God and I can only say to you – try and take your shoes off and offer them to others. But not just your shoes alone, we have so much that we really must offer it to our neighbour. There is so much varnish on our faces, there are so many things that stop atheists from believing in Jesus Christ because we are not ready to offer everything. There are many Christians, but very few are those ready to show the other cheek, and if they get slapped on one they argue by saying that this is not reasonable. It is not reasonable by human law, but it is by divine love. And the world is converted through people who love in this way – the Saints.

As long as we do not acquire this attitude, whereby we are prepared to offer even our tunic when robbed of our cloak, then we shall not be in a position to announce Jesus Christ. Therefore, I am asking you as well as myself to walk along this road of love, so that Christ may win.

As a last recommendation, I am telling you – have the courage to accept what Our Lady says and go and tell everybody, the whole world.

Tell them as well that, in order to announce peace, prayer and fasting, you do not need a passport, a special permit; on the contrary, « woe betide us if we do not announce it ».

Therefore, be brave and, if you like, I will say a prayer for you at the end. But first everyone please be seated.

I will explain why – it it right that your body should also rest; lean on the seats, if you like, so that you can feel just as if you were in the arms of your Heavenly Father. Go and meet, in your thoughts, the people with whom you have to reconcile yourselves, go to these people and say, « I forgive you », « I love you ». Let there be no deceit in your thoughts; if you want to prove your forgiveness you must take your brand new shoes off, offer these people something, give them a sign of your love. Do it in your hearts, make up your minds. I shall pray for you, for your needs.

Meanwhile, invoke in your hearts: «Jesus, Jesus, Jesus come. Jesus I want it, I have decided, give me this gift».
While the priest prays, let your hearts be active.

O Mother, most loving and sweet Mother, Queen of Peace, to you we consecrate our hearts, our minds, our souls. To you we consecrate our families, our sick, our church throughout the world. Help us now to obtain the graces Jesus Christ wants to give us. O Jesus come! Come amongst us and listen to our prayers.
I beg you, O Lord Jesus Christ, do not just listen to our prayers, but also look at the deepest needs in our hearts, as well as in our bodies. Come Lord Jesus! Lord Jesus Christ, we are leprous and often do not know why. Surely it must be because we have embarked on the wrong way, because we have adopted a false spiritual attitude. Free us from this wrong path and give us the good heart of peace. Come Lord Jesus!
We are full of bitterness, that is why we are unhappy and we forget to ask you to remove this bitterness from us, so now we beg you – take it away, O Lord! Also take away any worry and grant us your peace.
Come Lord Jesus!
Lord Jesus Christ we want you amongst us. Unfortunately every day we desire things and pleasures and you are often last; now we wish you to be first, come Lord Jesus!
Lord, many people are not even capable of praying to you because they have been disappointed, they are full of bitterness because they have been offended; heal all the broken hearts, open them to your mercy.
Lord Jesus Christ, look at the reason why these people have come to ask you graces. You know it well. If your will is to heal people – heal them. If your will is that the people should bear their crosses, help them to do so.
Lord Jesus Christ, look at all these people with their sicknesses and worries. With your hand touch every person, every wound, every sickness and heal it.
Lord Jesus Christ, you have offered everything for us, you can do

everything – open our hearts to your love and to the love of all men so that our prayer may be answered.

Lord Jesus Christ, give us your Holy Spirit, the spirit of joy, love, peace, prayer, patience – Come Holy Spirit!

O Jesus Christ, I beg you especially that this group may receive the message of your love and bring it to everyone. I beg you that your messages and those of your Mother may be in the hearts of these people, but that they may also be visible on the faces of these people, in their behaviour, so that those who meet them may be aware of a new life.

Lord Jesus Christ, I pray to you for all members of our families, for all the sick. I also pray to you at this moment for all the Church and all the people who are responsible for the Church, for all those responsible for the world, for all those who are starving, for all drug addicts, for all those who are unhappy; please Lord Jesus Christ, you who are love can at this moment touch every person – do it Lord Jesus Christ!

And I beg of you remain with us and increase these graces, so that the message of your Mother may grow and bear the fruits of salvation. Lord Jesus Christ, heal the sick, strengthen the weak, comfort the afflicted, grant your peace to all those who are worried and may your blessing be upon us and the whole world.

In the name of the Father, of the Son and of the Holy Spirit. Amen.

(Fr. Tomislav Vlašić - 29 July 1985)

I must wish to be like Jesus

I have good news for you. You have come here wishing to find something, but far more than you wish awaits you here, provided you open your hearts – God always offers us far more than we expect. The problem is that we are not open and come still worried about something, we want to retain something for ourselves, we come with our own plans. And God, as it were, is left with no room to manoeuvre within us. That is why I am telling you to-day – first of all long for the Kingdom of God. What does that mean? Above all, ask for any bitterness, any worry about things, about your families and everything that harasses you to be removed from you. If you are able to remove everything, then you are able to let God work within yourselves and you will attain the divine love and, through that, everything else will be granted to you.

At this point I will tell you about my experience. We Christians say many prayers, but, unfortunately, do not pray. We are people who say many prayers, not knowing what to ask God or what we should ask for. In my prayer, however, I must know what I want. What I ask for should become, first of all, the wish to become what the Gospel says. I must wish to be like Jesus. Read the Gospel, agree with every word in the Gospel. When your wishes become the wishes of Jesus Christ, then they will be met, then you will be able to obtain what Jesus Christ has promised. Something else I have learnt here. We Christians ask God, « I want this, I want that »; however, we are incapable of receiving. It happens to us exactly as happened to the eldest son of the parable, the one who stayed at home whilst the prodigal one had gone away. The eldest was at home, but, nevertheless, did not know how to take what was his own, he was incapable of making use of what he possessed.

The most important thing in prayer is knowing how to receive, but unfortunately, we do not want to receive. We say, « Our Father, thy Kingdom come... », but do not want his Kingdom. We say, « Thy will be done... », instead, we want to do our own will. We say, « Forgive us our trespasses as we forgive... », but do not want to forgive. Therefore, we do not want to receive. When we pray in such a way so as to do in practice what we say in words, then we will be able to receive all the graces. They will all be at our disposal. Whereas, if we do not put into practice the words of the Gospel, the ones contained in the Our Father, we will not be in a position to receive anything at all. There, you can see now how easy it is to succeed in obtaining. We only need to accept with simplicity the very simple words we say in our daily prayers or what we hear at Mass.

And if you want to know how one gets to moving mountains with the prayer of faith, you must set off with concrete steps, you must live those words more and more. You see, something terrible can happen – the word can be taken away from our heart and then it cannot produce fruit. There are people, Jesus explains, who listen to the word, but who allow themselves to be robbed straightaway of it by satan, like the seed fallen on the road and taken away by the birds. Let us be careful. If we go to church and we listen to the Word of the Lord, but do not live it, we have allowed satan to rob us; that is something terrible. If we do not receive this word addressed to us by the priest, by our father, by our mother, how can we possibly obtain fruit, if we have not even planted the divine Word? I now beg you to apply yourselves to receive with simplicity and humility every Word of God, day by day, and to allow it to grow.

I want to remind you of the message given by Our Lady on Maundy Thursday 1984, « *To-day I will disclose to you a spiritual secret. If you want to become stronger than evil, pray enough in the morning, read a passage of the Gospel and plant the divine Word in your hearts. Later on, during the day, often remember that Word, long for it and allow it to grow – in the evening you will be stronger that in the morning* ». In real terms, if you are impatient, find a word that heals your impatience. Are you the sort of person who often bears bitterness? Find the word that teaches you to forgive. Let it grow during the day and in this way you will practise a continuous resurrection, during the day. If this continuous process of growth is not in us, we cannot progress in the Gospel. To-day we have seen so many Christians, but when we see a Christian after ten years, do we see in him more of a Christian or the same as before? More of a saint or the same? Often, the same. If, during the lapse of ten years, a Christian has not grown, if he has not become more saintly, this is a tragedy for Christianity. So the message loses strength. I therefore invite you to welcome the divine word this evening.

Try and find some silence, put all these words into your hearts and decide to pray every day, as Our Lady tells us. Every morning plant the divine word that heals, let it grow during the day, then you will understand that you will have received to-day far more than you had wished for. You will then slowly enter into friendship with God and your neighbour and you will live in love.

Then you will not need to ask for so many things any more. They will be offered to you, you will find them already obtained. Christ will come towards you, he will be all for you.

(Fr. Tomislav Vlašić - 2 August 1985

« Open yourselves to God and God will be able to act through you »

The most important message here is the presence of Our Lady – already for fifty months – every evening.

Some people wonder – why for so long? Why? For me, this element of time becomes evidence of authenticity. If it had only been a question of fifteen days or fifty days someone might have said, « We could not carry out our research and, therefore, do not know exactly what went on ». But every kind of research possible has been done and both science and medicine have told us, « For us it is inexplicable ». The visionaries, though, have quite a simple explanation to give. « We see Our Lady ». They do not explain, but say, « We see ». All those who have opened their hearts know who is speaking.

Every Thursday Our Lady gives us a message through Marija, but she appears every night. And this is a message in itself. Our Lady is present, as the mother; she greets us through the visionaries, she will also bless us to-night. Through the visionaries she blesses us, our sick, even our objects. She is with us.

Because of her presence one can also explain the other happenings – a new spirit of prayer, of penance, of faith and also of reconciliation, of peace. These days, in her last messages, Our Lady mentions satan a great deal. In her last message, she said a phrase that we cannot fully understand – She asked us to pray, because satan had seized part of the project and is trying to win it for himself. We must pray that satan does not succeed in this.

This is an invitation, even though we do not quite know how satan can possibly act this way; it is very important to hear that we have to pray.

In another message she asked us to have many things blessed, to keep them in our homes and take them with us as a shield against satan. A very important message as an indication of satan's work, is the one of a month ago, when she said, « *I love you and protect this parish from any of satan's work. I invite you to pray for the parish so that satan may go away and that he also may leave alone anybody who comes to the parish* ». All this to enable us to hear the call.

In my opinion, this is the main, most important point, since it seems to me that according to this message, the first deed of satan's is to prevent the call from being heard. I am telling you that the main point in all this is not who speaks or who the visionaries are and how they live, but what really counts is the message, the fulfilment of the message. The message is, for us all – peace and reconciliation.

We are all somehow in danger of letting ourselves be prevented from listening. All those who say: « I am waiting for the authentication by the Church », do well. Personally, I am waiting for it, too. But if someone waiting for such an acknowledgement also waits for peace, reconciliation, prayer, fasting, faith, what is he doing? Many people have probably run this risk – they have not followed. Of this, I must say, I am a witness; many people here, perhaps everyone, open themselves to peace in a particular way. I have given some thought as to why. Probably, because the visionaries talk of peace and reconciliation frankly.

You see, when a head of government says « peace », people think – this must be diplomacy, he is perhaps after something. When, therefore, people hear, in different circles, the word « peace », they do not trust it.

Here, on the other hand, one talks simply, without diplomacy and this word « peace » can only be pronounced by heaven, through the visionaries, through the little ones, the simple ones, those who do not understand a thing of the world's diplomacy. It is this word the human heart is waiting for. And I see each one of us open, wanting peace and reconciliation. It is, however, very dangerous, if we get hindered by something, if we find an excuse from starting with prayer, with fasting. Why is prayer and fasting all important as a means – they are the path, the way to reach the source.

Our Lady does not ask prayer of us to make us waste time, she does not require fasting because it makes her happy to see us starve. None of this; with fasting and prayer, we are dealing with two means we should avail ourselves of in order to gain peace, to open ourselves to peace. And so she asks for the daily reciting of the Creed, seven Our Father's, the whole Rosary, the reading of the Bible. She then asks for fasting twice a week and monthly confession.

Why all this? These are all simple things, and I am absolutely convinced that she asks this of us in order to help us, so that we do not find excuses once again; we can all start or, we can carry on. And so every day our prayer develops. And if it happens to you, as in the case of St. Francis, to start the Our Father and end up praying just the Our Father all night long and you experience that sweetness in your mouths and some warmth in your hearts, you do well, you do more than Our Lady asks. This is a school of faith for us. But one must start right from the very simple things. I am telling you again, Our Lady does not ask for one hundred and fifty Hail Mary's – what can happen if someone understands that Our Lady asks for one hundred and fifty Hail Mary's? He will take up the Rosary and, in fifteen minutes will have said them all and will say, « I have finished for to-day, thank God ».

This is not the point, but, rather by praying the rosary, one is drawn nearer to Jesus, one lives with Jesus, with Our Lady in every situation of the day – when at work, at meal times, with one's family, always.

This does not mean to say that one can always pray, but one can certainly pray more often than one thinks. If someone smokes, say twenty cigarettes a day, and does not find a room to smoke in on his own, he is prepared to smoke in a factory where hundreds of others are smoking too, thus polluting the air. He smokes and is not ashamed of it. We, instead, when it comes to praying, say we cannot. So you see how we seem to have lost the sense of being close to Jesus, of being close to Our Lady. As Our Lady said, if you cannot find time for the whole rosary in your own home, because you have to get up early in the morning and come back late at night, you can still pray when driving your car, you can steal twenty minutes for the rosary, as you would for your coffee or cigarettes. As far as I can see, it is not a matter of time, but, instead, what above all is lacking, is the sense of the value of prayer. And so Our Lady asks for prayer in order to invite us to be close to Jesus.

And now to the question, « Is it important to be close to Jesus or not? ». Our Lady said, « *Pray and you will have the deepest joy, you will have peace, you will overcome your tiredness, you will also become handsome and beautiful. You will also have the strength for reconciliation* ».

So, on this point, we can afford to be really selfish – if we live close to Jesus, close to Our Lady, in God, we shall have the joy even when in suffering, we shall have peace and be able to bring peace, reconciliation, where others only create conflicts. From whom can one ever hope for peace in this world, where people make conflicts, if not from Christians? But just look at how far we are from this wisdom of the Cross and of Jesus.

I have just said that we can allow ourselves to be selfish – if you pray you will have your joy, you will overcome your tiredness, you will solve your problems. What does it mean, when Our Lady says that you will overcome your tiredness? Who is tired? He is tired who says, « I cannot ». Where there is divorce in a family this is a sign of tiredness in to-day's world. A family who cannot solve its own problems and is in conflict is a tired family. A youngster who is on drugs, or drinks, is a tired person. And there are many of those in the world. Our Lady says, « *Pray and you will overcome your tiredness* ». When I say that prayer is a means to become beautiful, I am not joking.

Jelena once asked Our Lady, « Why are you so beautiful? ». The answer was, « *I am beautiful because I love. If you want to be beautiful, love* ». This is a deeply theological message – we are all created according to God's image, all handsome and beautiful, full of peace.

This is the reflection of heaven – being reconciled with the Lord and all others. When sin came into the life of the human race, into our life, it ruined our soul, our hearts. One must pray, open oneself, because thanks to the gift of grace and love one becomes good-looking, created to God's image.

One must say though, that if, as it stands, outer beauty partially depends on inner beauty, it is perhaps easier to decide in favour of this inner beauty, of the love the Lord offers us.

So, the answer to my question, « Is it very important to be close to Jesus or not? » is, « Yes, as we can receive everything ».

In the message before last, Our Lady said, « *Open yourselves, the Lord wants to work through you and give you all that is necessary* », in other words – if we are left without peace these days, in these times of grace, if we are left without reconciliation, it is because we have remained closed and so the Lord cannot give himself to us.

If we remain poor in this respect, it is because of our sin. Once again I will draw a comparison – quite an important one – just so that we can see what Our Lady wants these days. One day She said, « *I am saved, but I also want you to be saved* ». That is to say, this is again meant for us.

I spoke to a theologian who saw a parallel between Medjugorje and Fatima, and said, « seventeen years from the beginning of this century there was a great appeal to mankind – conversion, penance, prayer. What happened next? Just think of World War II and so many other terrible things. Seventeen or eighteen years before the end of the same century, again, a great appeal which has been going on for fifty months – be converted, be reconciled, peace. Who will be responsible if terrible things come again? Who will be able to say, "I did not know? Can I really wash my hands of it"? ».

For this very reason I have asked you to mark the difference between the acknowledgement of the apparition and the acknowledgement of the invitation to prayer and peace. At the end of the apparitions I asked Ivanka, « Ivanka, what shall I tell the pilgrims? Should I speak of fear or of hope? ». She replied, « Of hope, Our

Lady did not come here to condemn, but to save us ». And She will be able to save us if we give her our hand. She told us, « *I want to guide you, but you are still not listening. Open yourselves, God wants to operate through you and give you all that is necessary* ». These days, if you want to give Our Lady a wonderful present, all She needs is your hand and mine – let yourselves be guided. She will then certainly be full of joy, if allowed to lead us to Jesus. And step by step She will manage and I believe She will not leave us in peace until She has once again gathered all her sons and daughters into her home. As the Bible says, She is a strong woman. So, we had better start immediately.

For a moment let us just consider one of Jelena's visions, in order to capture once more the meaning of these messages. One and a half months ago Jelena saw a splendid pearl. Soon after it appeared it split into parts and each of these parts tended to shine a little and then die out. Our Lady's explanation was the following, « *Jelena, every man's heart which belongs totally to God is like this splendid pearl; it shines even in darkness. But when it is shared a little with satan, a little with sin, a little with everything, then it dies out and it is not worth anything anymore* ».

Our Lady wants us to belong totally to the Lord without reserve without showing ourselves to be wiser than Jesus Christ, than Our Lady. She wants us to take their path and to live it. If we do this, we stand to lose nothing; on the contrary, we receive peace, reconciliation, love.

Behind this vision, we find basically the same concept – although in different words – as when She invited us to say the Creed every day. That we must not say it as a formula we have known since the days of our religious instruction but rather to « give our hearts ». Creed means decision. This is prayer.

You must start to fast. You can read the full explanation about this in the book, « Open your Hearts to Mary Queen of Peace ». There you will also find the explanation of other things.

There is so much one could say on fasting, but the main thing is to start and then you will see.

(Fr. Slavko Barbarić - 4 August 1985)

« Many a time I have given you my blessing and you have lost it »

I will give you a summary of the news.

The most remarkable feature in the messages during the month of July is that Our Lady often warned us on the reality of satan and invited us to pray a lot in order to drive him away from this place and from all the pilgrims who come here. Our Lady specially advised people to have sacred objects blessed, to wear them and to put them in their homes as a protection against satan.

Lately, She said that satan had decided to seize part of her plan and destroy it, and so She asked us to pray, so that he may not succeed. Through other visionaries, Jelena and Marijana – who have locutio interna – Our Lady carries on talking and imparting messages. A particular message has come through Jelena, in which Our Lady has again warned us on the reality of satan.

For all these reasons Our Lady urges us to take our spiritual weapons – fervent prayer, humility, sincerity, mutual love, and, as She once said, « *Satan will not even be able to come anywhere near you* ».

The visionaries tell us that, during the apparitions, Our Lady renews, always in different words, her appeal for prayer, fasting, conversion, in order to gain peace.

I would now like to bring to your attention something that will help you live this reality. Lately I read about an episode, some of you might know of, on that preacher in Korea. He had been sick for eighteen years and the doctors had to discharge him from hospital as they had lost all hope of saving him. He was a Buddhist, and during his illness, a Christian girl used to come and visit him every day and talk to him about Jesus. At the sound of this preaching the young man used to get bored and eventually said to the girl. « Go away, I do not wish to listen to you ». Kneeling down, the girl began to cry and to beg Jesus to save this man. After these tears were shed, the young man said to her, « Do not cry, I will get baptized, because you love me ». Afterwards, the young man explained that, whilst the girl was crying, it became very clear in his soul that Jesus Christ is really the Saviour. He decided to be baptized, he offered his life to Jesus Christ, after which he was suddenly healed.

He is now the preacher of a parish with three hundred thousand souls and in his parish many signs are known to take place. Pay attention then – to a girl who wanted to save a man, after praying there was nothing left but to cry in front of God – she managed to save a person who now has the task of guiding three hundred thousand people to Jesus Christ.

Please be like this in the face of God. You will be going back to your homes to-night, to-morrow, the day after to-morrow; be determined, right from to-night to really save people. Go home with a firm mind to go and save people and set out on the road as this girl – announce Jesus Christ, pray, and, if you are not capable of converting people, cry with a heart full of love and you will save those people.

If we are not in a position to go and save people, neither can we understand Our Lady's presence, since Our Lady cried many times through the ages in order to save us, and we cannot understand the apparitions of Lourdes, Fatima or the ones of Medjugorje either, if we are incapable of grasping this message, of being stirred to go and save other people. But we shall not be able to save others if we do not do something inside ourselves. A week ago, through Jelena, Our Lady gave us another message, « *For the next few days I want you to bring your full attention to this thought: – it has been a long, long time since I met my friend Jesus, it has been a long, long time since I met my mother Mary; in these days I want to meet them both* ».

It is a very simple message, but at the same time a very deep one indeed. When we have a friend, a son, a daughter, we do not get into a crisis in order to love them. A mother is capable of staying up all night, every night by her sick daughter's bed, because inside her there is love. If you are able to love Jesus Christ, to love his Mother, you will have courage, you will have light, you will have everything in your hearts to enable you to follow Our Lady and also to understand her. You will have the courage to face all problems. At the same time, if you have this friendship with Jesus Christ, you will sense salvation within you. Unfortunately, many of us Christians have never even met Jesus Christ the friend; we might have come across some God who is there to impose order and we just perform our Christian duties under obligation. As long as our heart is not stirred by friendship, by love, we cannot possibly be apostles, be witnesses to others. I urge you to make friends with Christ. One cannot make friends with Jesus Christ if one's heart is not fully open. You only know too well how we feel with a friend – time flies, but one never grows tired of him. On the other hand, we are not even capable of being with Jesus Christ for five minutes; we are in a hurry and it does seem a long time. This is just an example to show that we are not friends of Jesus Christ yet. But if we are friends of Jesus Christ, friends of Our Lady, then we can easily spend a long time and rest with Jesus Christ.

With regard to this, I would like to tell you – take Our Lady and Saint Joseph and go with them; it is symbolical, but it is also real. May your morning be like Our Lady's – just like Our Lady was so open before the angel – in this way, every morning, in a fairly long prayer, open yourselves totally to God. So when I say, « open yourselves totally to God », try and meet God, and I mean meet Him, as Our Lady told us many a time in Her messages, « *In every prayer it is necessary to hear God's voice, to meet God, so do try every morning to offer and abandon all your difficulties, all people, to God, so that throughout the day you will be free from all worry and will experience a dependance on God and feel as light as a child* ».

If you start your day this way with Our Lady, you will see the results during the day. In the evening, close your day with St.

Joseph. It is very beautiful, for as we can read in the Scriptures, messages used to come to St. Joseph in his sleep, and not only in his sleep, but in his dreams. Mankind of to-day thinks of other things in its sleep; in one's sleep, fears, problems, sin, tend to arise. St. Joseph received his message even in his sleep and if you, at night, abandon your hearts totally to God, if you manage to slip into your sleep free from the burden of any sin, then there is room for God, for him to even speak to you in your sleep, in order to prepare your next day. Follow, therefore, Our Lady and St. Joseph. Without this rhythm of prayer of at least morning and evening, you will not succeed in living your days with God. People who are devoted to prayer need more frequent encounters during the day.

My advice to you – Take at least these two steps a day – every morning, so that you may become totally abandoned to God and in the evening unload all difficulties and sins. I then ask you to take a step forward on leaving this church. You often come here asking for miracles. It is easy, quite easy to obtain the miracle; however the road one normally takes is difficult and one does not succeed in attaining it. Many people ask for a miracle like jumping over a mountain, but it is not so in spiritual life.

For a believer, one achieves impossible things through possible steps. So if you want to start to-night – open the Bible and put into practice the first line you read. It is the first step, start putting into practice the words you have heard a thousand times before and you have not accepted. If you have skipped those very simple words you will not reach the miracle, but if you go along the path of this simplicity, practising these very simple words, when you take a step, God will show you another and another.

In this way you will reach the mountain, you will attain the things that seem impossible. One achieves the impossible through faith. There is something terrible in the parable of the sower – Jesus talks about the seed that fell on the road. The birds came and took it away. In giving an explanation, Jesus says, « Those are the believers who have welcomed the word and allowed satan to take it away ».

If you leave this church and do not welcome the word, then you have sweated in vain, you get robbed by satan. He has taken away from you all you have earned for yourselves, all you have laboured and toiled for. Mind satan does not steal all you earn, every day; this is something extremely simple, but at the same time, heroic and tragic.

It is heroic, if we, day in day out, put every word into practice, no matter how small it may be and heroic, also because we will at some stage achieve great things. It is, however, tragic if we lose everything God gives us at Mass, in prayer, at the moment of our labour.

In a message Our Lady told us more or less this, « *When I am far away, you shout asking for help, when I give you the gift you lose it immediately* ».

The reproach I have heard through the visionaries during these last four years, the deepest expression of sorrow, is the one Our Lady pronounced in her blessing: « *So many times I have given you my blessing and you have lost it* ». If you intend to reach the spiritual depths and go further in your spiritual life, then you must pay attention to all these small details. I say small, but in reality they are big. You cannot get to Mostar from here in one step; similarly, you cannot see Rome from here but, in order to get there you must take a whole sequence of small steps. Thus one reaches impossible things, as it were, because in God there are no impossible things. If we take these practical steps everyday, then God will explain everything to us. It is most important what I am telling you – if you follow these footsteps there will be no fanatics among you, as fanatics are a problem for Jesus Christ as well as for Our Lady.

If you follow these steps, then there will not be so many pilgrims saying, « Ask Our Lady to explain this and that »; it will be God, it will be Our Lady who will explain everything within our hearts. However, as we do not take these concrete steps in the light of the Holy Spirit, we are unable to interpret what God is telling us.

That is why we must take these practical steps – so that we can reach the light which grows stronger every day.

Thus we will be able to announce the messages to others and what must happen to us, dear pilgrims, is what happened to the Samaritans, when the Samaritan woman proclaimed having met the Messiah. The Samaritans came and said, « Now we know, not because you have told us, but because we know ».

So therefore, through prayer, deep prayer we will attain a light and confidence, like the confidence which the visionaries possess with their hearts.

We must obtain a tangible inner confidence, the confidence of faith through prayer. A kind of confidence whereby all things are made clear to us. Therefore, I am telling you – set out on the path of simplicity. Every day we must enter into the light in order to reach a complete light.

In practice, what I want to underline is this – in the prayer group Our Lady imparts certain messages – she does not give them just for the sake of saying them, but tells us, « This week you must practise this message, this Lent you must practise this other message ».

Within our prayer group we spent the second half of Lent just practising the Our Father; we did nothing else but pray the Our Father for hours on end, just enter into the true prayer of the Our Father, to pray with our hearts, so as to reach the light and depth of Our Father. So now you see, Our Lady has granted us some prayers, has prompted us to read the Gospel, to say the Rosary. I am inviting you not only to say the Rosary, but to improve it. Let us not say any longer, « In the second joyful mystery we commemorate the visit of Our Lady to her cousin Elizabeth, Our Father who art in heaven, hallowed be... ». This is no reflection, this is no contemplation; one has to stop the machine, one has to ponder, enter. Try and apply yourselves for one day, all day, to just say Hail Mary, repeating the first part. So on the first day repeat just the first part; on the second day just the second part, again all day long, or the Our Father, in order to enter its depth. When you will have entered the depth of prayer, then you will see, as Our Lady said in a message, Our Father becomes an easy inner melody, leading us to joy, happiness.

Now then, I will finish with the prayer of blessing for you all, for the sacred objects, the ordinary objects and the sick.

Lord Jesus Christ, I beg you, through the Virgin Mary, Queen of Peace to send your blessings on all the pilgrims. Lord, you see all their difficulties, but know our prime difficulty is the impediment we feel in our hearts to meet you as a friend.

Lord Jesus Christ, help us experience your friendship this evening, to experience the Motherhood of the Virgin Mary.

Lord Jesus Christ, open all hearts to your words, prompt us all to practise every word of yours which is written in the Gospel, help us in real life, to carry out your plan of love.

Lord Jesus Christ, free all those souls which are full of bitterness, of anguish, of worry, of sin.

Open them to your presence.

Lord, heal all souls, heal also the sick in body.

Bless all our families, all parishes, all communities, all Italy. Bless the whole church and the whole world.

You are the only friend who can save us.

Save us, Lord Jesus Christ!

And I beg you, bless all sacred objects and let them be our defence and protection from any negative influence.

And I bless you, in the name of the Father, of the Son, and of the Holy Spirit. Amen.

(Fr. Tomislav Vlašić - 5 August 1985)

The moment of prayer is the moment of the transfiguration of the soul

Welcome.

I have a few minutes to devote to you. I shall only say a few words; you are, however, filled with graces, you have just arrived from Medjugorje, you have prayed and I do not want to repeat the news you heard last night, instead, would like to tell you something else – you all wish to know God, to know Our Lady. First of all I believe that each one of us wishes to see Our Lady as the visionaries see her – you can see her in different ways. An Austrian writer who lived in Latin America for a long time says in one of his novels that the most beautiful thing in the world are his mother's eyes on Friday night. Why? Because on Fridays she prays and fasts a lot. Two are the means to attain inner transparency – prayer and fasting.

Our Lady continuously invites us to pray and fast in order to accomplish this inner purity.

Then we can meet Our Lady and meet God. But this reality I am talking about is a reality for which only a few want to meet Our Lady or God. Everybody would like to see the outer signs – you heard last Sunday that outer signs do not save us, since Jesus said, « Search for me, not because you have seen the signs, but because you have eaten the bread I have offered you ».

This inner transparency, this inner purity, leads us to the very inner sight of God. It is a state of soul in prayer. If our prayers do not end up allowing us to see God, experience God, meet God, such prayers are not successful. And every prayer, all fasting, every form of prayer and fasting ought to bring us to this attitude – see God, meet God, find and reach an inner purity, a certainty; when everything is comprehensible, everything is clear, when we can do everything according to divine power.

Achieving this clarity is worth more than seeing Our Lady the way the visionaries see her, since they have to strive to reach this clarity, the same way as we have to. The deepest realities of the visions are the virtues – faith, hope, love. Attaining this blossoming of the soul means attaining the very aim of our faith – the unity with God. Try and practise faith and the messages Our Lady has given us.

There is no point in our going to Medjugorje a thousand times if we do not try and fulfill those messages in a simple, most simple manner, in order to reach this state of soul. The only thing that counts in spiritual life is to enter into friendship with God; when we are close to Him and everything in our soul is open to Him, then God is able to build everything within us. And so, the small things that bother us daily do not bother us any longer; it is God who gives us life.

I want to tell you this to-day, as the church celebrates the Transfiguration of Jesus on the mountain. As you very well know, the Transfiguration did not take place at the stadium or in the street, but in the silence of the mountain, after a long prayer Jesus had with some chosen friends – the Apostles Peter, John and James. He retired to the silence of prayer and then the Transfiguration took place.

This is not just a sign for us, but an indication as to how we can reach this inner, spiritual Transfiguration through prayer; through a kind of prayer, however, where we are not the ones to do the talking – at least, not the only ones, to show God the ways, to show God our wishes – but rather, prayer is the moment in which we allow God to act in us, to change us.

I was impressed by the experience of an Italian doctor who was here a month ago. He told us that during these last few years he has become aware of having been caught up in a certain vicious circle – I just rush, rush, rush, forgetful of my family and of God. Not that I am against God, but I am just not able to stop, to stay in front of God. So, he said, I prayed thus, « O God stop me! Send me

some trial or I shall be lost, since I am not capable of stopping ».
A few months later he had a paralysis and said, « When I received
this affliction and was in hospital, I then remembered my prayer
and was pleased about it. So, paralysed as I was, I was putting
myself in front of God, pondering and seeking to abandon myself
totally to God, to start a new life. And as I was letting myself go
inwardly, so was the ailment disappearing. A few months later I
was healed and came to Medjugorje to thank God for having given
me this affliction ». It is very important that we place ourselves
before God, totally open and abandoned, also with our prayer
« God, as I am not capable of walking, take me by the hand. If I
am incapable of stopping this rushing, stop me, help me, send me
even trials ». The moment of prayer is the moment of the transfiguration of the soul, we must therefore be prepared to put everything on the Cross, since only if the old self dies shall we be
transformed. We must allow Jesus to operate this transformation,
this transfiguration of our souls.

There, my wish is that you may follow these messages, mostly by
means of a continuous, daily, silent and deep prayer in order to
be transformed.

And it would be nice, very nice indeed if people were to say of you,
« the best thing I saw today were the eyes of that man I met in
the street ». If we were thus to be witnesses before people, soon
the world would be changed, transfigured. Try and do it, so as to be
witnesses of the transfiguration of Jesus in your hearts. For this I
will give you my blessing. I would like to ask you something
else – usually, after the community blessing there are some who
wish for a special blessing. This is often a sign that you do not
take the blessing given during Mass into due consideration. Be
prepared, therefore, to receive the blessing when God gives you the
blessing; He gives it to you as much as you want, without rationing;
He is a good Father. Be recollected now so that you may be ready
to receive this blessing.

Lord Jesus Christ, You chose Peter, James and John to pray with
when on Mount Tabor, and You were transfigured. You have
called these people to Medjugorje, You have called them to a

deeper prayer. Through the Holy Spirit O Lord may these people be transfigured. Take away any bitterness, all aggressiveness, all depression, all worry from their souls. O Lord Jesus Christ, may you take away any anxiety to earn and to succeed in life. Change family and personal situations, any ailment of the soul, any sin, and also, if you so wish, any physical illness. Ensure, Lord Jesus Christ, that the eyes and the souls of the people gathered here may be transfigured, so that they may be witnesses of Your presence and of the presence of Your Mother.

Lord Jesus Christ, may you transfigure their relatives, their parishioners, their friends and their enemies. Let the whole country be transfigured.

Lord Jesus Christ You have been transfigured amongst the apostles to be revealed to the whole world, let the entire Church, together with the Pope, our Bishop and all the representatives be transfigured and be a sign to the world, just as your Mother Mary is a sign to the Church; may the whole world be saved.

And I bless you in the name of the Father, of the Son and of the Holy Spirit. Amen.

I ask you especially in these days to pray for Medjugorje, for Our Lady's intention as expressed by Her in Her last message. Satan has decided to take a hold of part of Her plan in order to destroy it. Therefore, pray that Our Lady's plan may not be destroyed, but that it may come to fruition.

Best wishes and have a good journey.

(Fr. Tomislav Vlašić - 6 August 1985)

Continue to grow in peace, in reconciliation, in love

The apparitions now last sometimes three, four or five minutes as Our Lady wishes. Vicka, Marija, Ivan, Jakov have daily apparitions and always pray for peace and for all pilgrims, with Our Lady; they ask the blessing for the sick and also for sacred objects. What does Our Lady want from us? The first message is the presence of Our Lady. When I asked Ivanka, « What shall I tell the pilgrims? ». « Shall I talk about fear or hope? ».

« Of hope, since Our Lady has come not to condemn us, but to save us ». So you see, Our Lady is present and from Her presence one can explain all that has been happening here for the last fifty months. It is a very exceptional thing, but as far as we are concerned, a very common and daily happening. Our Lady asks for peace, conversion, faith, prayer, fasting, as guidelines of our life and, more specifically, She asks for the daily Creed, for seven Our Father's, for the whole Rosary, complete with the three parts – joyful, sorrowful and glorious – for the reading of the Bible, to fast twice a week and confession once a month.

These are the concrete things Our Lady is asking of us. She obviously asks us to pray with all our hearts, to make time for prayer, to become active in prayer and to ensure that our Mass becomes a live experience of God. However, in all this, Our Lady asks us to open ourselves to prayer, to Our Lord's invitation, to this invitation of peace, reconciliation – She wants to save us. And all the other Thursday messages are stimuli for us to stick to the path with Our Lady.

During these days I want to mention one thing – Peace. Every day, for the last fifty months, Our Lady has been praying with the visionaries for peace and we are all invited to peace.

The visionaries say, « peace, reconciliation » and only repeat the words our Mother asks them to pass on to us. And I can honestly say, according to my own experience here in Medjugorje of the last forty months, that many hearts, if not all, who having got here and started to pray and fast, have actually felt this call, this invitation to peace. Only Heaven and no one else in this world can pronounce the word peace, can invite us to peace, to the degree where we can believe that peace is actually possible.

Judging by what is happening here with us, I think I can quite honestly say that on the spiritual front, the one of faith, the messages have been accepted as being messages of the Gospel and has also accepted their practice.

After this appeal who will be able to say, « I have been waiting ». What for? You see, it is fifty months now, and I think I am in a position to say that the longer it lasts, the firmer I am in my conviction that it must be a strong appeal for us all. As far as we can gather from here, this message is spreading to the whole world and Our Lady has already found many a soul even within other churches, that is the Anglican, Protestant and Baptist churches.

An Anglican vicar spent three weeks here and said, « I have understood one thing – Our Lady is not asking my conversion to the Catholic Church, but that I improve myself, as I too have the Gospel ». Last year he came back and said, « As I got back home, I started talking to my friends about it and – one wondered – how is it that so many people would listen with wide-open eyes. We formed nearly thirty prayer groups, all made up of Anglicans, Baptists, Protestants, Pentecostals with some members of these prayer groups being even Buddhists and atheists. They stated that if a Madonna is called Queen of Peace and invites us to pray, they too would join in and pray ».

And this is a great miracle for the Anglican who told me, « Father, you know there is not a great deal of room for Our Lady in our churches, as She has almost been chased out; She is now inviting us and this message is spreading ».

Look at the Thursday messages, one can say that Our Lady is inviting us to prayer in order to obtain the deepest joy, to solve difficulties, to overcome tiredness.

On this point we can really afford to become selfish; if you pray you will obtain your joy, you will overcome your tiredness, you will solve your problems. We are, therefore, allowed to become selfish. However, if we carry on growing in peace, reconciliation, spiritual strength, love, people will receive a lot from us, even the whole world.

One cannot expect this call to peace to come from others though, one must start from oneself and this is, somehow, the hardest way of going about it, as it is easier to invite others to patience rather than being patient oneself, it is easier to invite others to forgiveness than to forgive. We must start from ourselves. If we Christians start living the Gospel message Our Lady repeats here, the world will be closer to peace. And this is very important – that we should feel a little responsible for what is happening around, even though we are not heads of state, it does not matter; peace depends on all of us – from your prayer, from your behaviour.

And now some of yesterday's news:
... Ivanka was not present at the apparition, Jakov is in Sarajevo. To Vicka, Marija and Ivan Our Lady has appeared three times; once as She usually does, before Mass. They then went up to the hillside, as Our Lady appears there every Monday night, for their group only. To-day Marija told me that She appeared at half past eleven and again at midnight. On all three occasions She repeated that we must really be full of joy. They told me that She has blessed everyone in a special way.

She was joyful because so many people had come. Lately Our Lady has been asking the visionaries for some other prayers. She asked them to pray more « *until my birthday* ».

You can therefore feel a very close, very motherly and friendly presence. It does not seem strange to me any more if the visionaries come up to me and say, « The Queen of Peace says so and so... ». It is as if one who is amongst us were to say, « Do this, do that ». All those who come here and start to pray feel Her presence, hear Her voice.

(Fr. Slavko Barbarić - 6 August 1985)

« To the Lord of all hearts »

... When one talks to Mirjana one perceives that there are certain things which are drawing near, but when a visionary or a prophet says, « it will not be long now », we cannot possibly measure this in terms of days or months as we know them; it is the same as when in the Gospel Jesus says, « this generation will not be over that everything will come true »; but which generation? In any case, what we can say is that certain things will happen shortly. This is not for us to fear – this is rather, once again, for all of us, a call to accept the message, to pray and to fast as Our Lady asks.

I can and must say that satan's primary task is to stop us from hearing the Lord's call. I am always appealing to you to pay attention to this fact. Try to discern well what one should wait for and what not to wait for in order to get started.

So, therefore, all these messages, all these events have only one aim – Our Lady wants to take us by the hand and lead us to Jesus, to God.

In a message She said, « *To the Lord of all hearts* », so that we may have the peace, the strength for reconciliation, the deepest joy the world cannot give, that we may have faith, that we may truly live.

So many times I hear the question, « What Our Lady asks for is too much. How is it? How can we? We have our work to do, how can we pray the whole Rosary? ». It is certainly a permissible question and I have a general answer to it. « When we will have discovered the value of prayer, we shall also find the time for it ». For example, he who smokes wastes a little time; where does he get this time from? You may say that he is used to it, he needs to find some quiet, some peace through his cigarette. You see, we are used to seeing people smoking, but we have yet to discover prayer.

The whole world, all we possess cannot give us what the Lord gives us in prayer. And if so many are tired in this world, if there are many conflicts, many wars, if so many have nothing to eat (there are eight hundred million of them), if there are so many unhappy people with no aim in life, it is only because we do not pray, because we have sent the Lord away.

By inviting us to prayer, Our Lady wants us to rediscover the Lord and, with this, the opportunity to carry on living.

The Rosary is an appeal to be together with Our Lady and Jesus in everything. If we have grasped this, then we can take advantage of the Rosary, of the mysteries. By being close to Mary when She says yes to the Lord's will, when She visits others, when Jesus is born, when She presents Him to the Temple, we also learn about this life that Jesus has asked of us. If a mother tells her son, « You must take two hundred steps and, by so doing, we can spend two hours together » and that son replies, « My God, who can do two hundred steps a day? » he has forgotten that his mother invites him to be together. And the same goes for the Rosary. The Rosary is the biblical meditative prayer which takes us step by step, which takes even our heart and soul close to Jesus, to Our Lady. I was speaking yesterday to Marija, together with two priests, and they asked, « Does it seem a lot to you, that Our Lady should ask for the whole Rosary » Marija replied, « Not at all, when I see what is happening in the world, I could pray three times the whole Rosary ». Therefore, when we finally discover the value of prayer and when we start believing that prayer can actually help the whole world, then we shall find and have more time for prayer.

Why fasting? There is a lot to be said about this. I will explain how Our Lady asks us to fast – that it should be based on bread and water. This is the strictest, the ideal form. Obviously, if someone cannot, if one has problems with low blood pressure, then he is allowed some coffee.

If someone is ill, he will find his way. If someone has trouble fasting for two days, then he can start with one. However, this fasting is not an invitation to give up something. Our Lady invites us to live on bread for one day, to discover bread. If you start in this way you will once again discover the Eucharist and you will probably pay attention to the grace of faith; you will be able to pray more easily, you will detach yourselves a little from the material world and you will become freer in your hearts, even more transparent. And that is good for the soul and for the body. Medicine itself advises us to let our stomachs rest for a day.

If you do this, if you start, you will see what fasting means – it is very important. Fasting also helps faith and prayer. We must know that Jesus also fasted and so have all the prophets and saints. We Christians of this world do not want to bother with it.

The Church has established a minimum of two days in a year – Ash Wednesday and Good Friday, but that is the absolute minimum. We, instead, on these two days have dined better than usual by preparing a good fish dish.

Here is a call to rediscover fasting. In fact, the Fathers of the Church have said, « Fasting is the body's prayer »; it is prayer, but it also helps us to understand others. If someone feels a little hungry twice a week, he will more easily and deeply hear the voices of Africa and Asia crying out, « We have nothing to live on. We have no bread ».

A lot more can be said.

Starting with prayer and fasting, we give our hand to Our Lady, and Our Lady will be able to lead us to Jesus.

(Fr. Slavko Barbarić - 7 August 1985)

« I protect you with my cloak »

We must always ask ourselves why the apparitions are lasting so long. Maybe because we happen to be at a special time when the Lord wants to save us.

Our Lady gave us Her name, « *I am the Queen of Peace* ». We can therefore understand what She wants; She has asked of everyone – Peace, Reconciliation.

Marija Pavlović told us that on the third day of the apparitions she received a special vision – she saw Our Lady with a big black cross who repeated three times, « *Be reconciled* ».

So, the first important message for us all is the invitation to peace and reconciliation.

Once Our Lady said, « *Be converted to prayer. But you are not able to because your hearts are caught up by the material world* ». By fasting, in this case, we liberate ourselves and, step by step, we become freer. Prayer helps fasting and fasting helps prayer.

And this, whether we start it or carry on, is a radical move towards peace. I invite you on behalf of all the visionaries and of Our Lady with whom they talk, « *Open yourselves* ».

In the next few days you will receive new stimuli for your Christian life. So many have already taken up praying again, living peace. reconciliation. We pray for everyone and you, when you get home, pray for us.

To-day's message was, « *Dear children, to-day I call you especially to help Me fight against satan by means of prayer. Satan has decided to act more vigorously now that you are aware of his activity. Take up your arms against satan and with the Rosary in your hands defeat him. Thank you for responding to my call* ».

Our Lady once again invites us to fight against satan. Satan does not get weary and Our Lady invites us once again to take up our arms and pray the Rosary.

To-day is the feast of St. Dominic, maybe it is for this reason that She invites once again to the prayer of the Rosary.

For the last month, every Thursday, She has been inviting us to the battle against satan.

She wants to protect us so that She may bring to our lives the very fruits that satan wants to prevent us from having.

She once said, « *Do not be afraid of satan. There is no need for that, since one can easily disarm him with humble prayer and with burning love* ».

So with this hope Our Lady is with us.

In the message before last She said, « *I protect you with my cloak* ». She did not say, « I shall try and protect you », but She said, « *I protect you* ».

So we want to follow Her and go forward with Her in our life.

Now, go in peace, we shall meet again to-morrow. To everyone leaving now – « Peace ».

(Fr. Slavko Barbarić - 8 August 1985)

« Defeat satan with the Rosary in your hand »

Yesterday, Vicka, Marija and Ivan were present at the apparition — they prayed the Our Father, Hail Mary, Glory Be. At the second Our Father they knelt down, and the apparition lasted five minutes. In yesterday's message Our Lady invites us to fight against satan with prayer and said, « *Satan now knows you know he is active. Pray and defeat him with prayer, with the Rosary in your hands* ». For the last month, in nearly every message, Our Lady has been repeating, « *Beware of satan!* » and a theologian said, « The safest strategy of satan is when people say he does not exist and does not operate. When he is hidden he is capable of everything ».

But Our Lady has discovered him and therefore you can say he is angry and wants to act even more. But one need not be afraid of satan. Our Lady once told us, « *With fervent prayer, with humble love one can easily disarm him* », and promised She would protect us. In any case, if we stick to this path of faith, prayer and fasting, the Lord's project with us will triumph. His project is universal and personal.

If I allow sin to destroy my peace, my love, satan has already succeeded in destroying part of the Lord's projects, as the Lord wants us all to be saved.

And so here is a strong invitation to pray, fast and abandon ourselves in faith.

(Fr. Slavko Barbarić - 9 August 1985)

« I have been calling you to conversion for four years »

I greet you all, welcome.

I am well aware of the fact that on hot days such as these, it is not easy to embark on a pilgrimage, but surely, this is also a sign of your love for Our Lady and also of your wish to understand what peace means, what it means to carry it in one's heart and bring it to the world.

I will tell you what the position is with regard to the visionaries at present; I presume you have read a lot about it in books and newspapers. Then I want to talk about the spirituality of the messages, namely, what all this means or can mean to us.

You know that at the beginning the visionaries were six; since Christmas 1982, that is to say, one and a half years from the beginning of the apparitions, Our Lady has ended the daily apparitions with Mirjana and will now appear to her on her birthday. Mirjana is now having "locutio interna", which means that she hears the same voice she used to hear during the apparitions and says that, during these internal locutions, Our Lady talks to her and prays. She often tells her about the secrets and gives her new details and explanations.

To-day they were telling me that she received another locution last week, on the occasion of the feast of the Assumption.

Our Lady will again talk to her at the end of August. After the locution of the 1 June of this year, Mirjana has chosen Father Pero, chaplain and priest of the parish, as her confidant and she will one day confide to him the secret messages. Ten days before the coming of an event she will disclose it to him and he, in turn, will be allowed to tell it to the world three days beforehand.

So far, she has not told him anything and he does not know when and how she will tell him.

As far as Ivanka is concerned, her position is as follows: Our Lady has not been appearing to her since 7 May. However, Our Lady has promised She would appear to her on the anniversary of the apparitions, that is, on 25 June 1986. In this last apparition and the one before that, to Ivanka, should anybody try to look for something proving the authenticity of the apparitions, they can find it on a psychological level. Many have written or said that these are mere hallucinations or illnesses, but when one learns what Our Lady has said during the apparition, « *I am not coming any longer, I am coming next year* », and that Ivanka was very upset at the thought that She would not be coming any longer, this very detail can destroy all theories supporting hallucinations or other psychic illnesses.

Who is there who knows of any hallucinations saying, « I am not coming again? ».

It is quite clear, therefore, that we are dealing with a Person who allows Herself to be seen when She wants and Who withdraws when She wants. The visionaries are exposed to this "seeing", and they are not in a position to say « Let us pray, let us pray and we shall see Our Lady ». No, they do not do that, but start praying when they know Our Lady has promised to come. You can plainly see here, therefore, a total inner freedom in the hearts of the visionaries; they do not have to make an effort in order to see, in order to receive the apparition; they stay normal. All other theories must fall, they cannot corroborate these details, these witnesses of the visionaries.

On the other hand, it is already fifty months since this has been happening; we have also allowed experiments to take place; every experiment one could possibly undertake and the doctors' final conclusion has been: « We cannot explain what is happening ». Whereas the visionaries have been explaining from the beginning, « We see Our Lady ». This is very important in order to learn, to accept the message.

Vicka is now receiving the account of the world's future from Our

Lady; she is writing down everything, but it is still all a secret to us. From this one can understand that the apparitions are coming to an end, but we cannot measure things according to our days or months.

Mirjana told me, « Some of the events are coming close, and for this reason I have chosen a priest to confide in ». But when a visionary or prophet says things are close at hand or getting closer, this must be interpreted in the biblical sense, rather broadly, it cannot be gauged by our own means.

None of us ever expected, or could have even hoped for these apparitions to last this long.

Every Thursday Marija Pavlović conveys to us a message from Our Lady. We shall see what it will be to-day. Our Lady is telling Jakov about the future of the world; Ivan does not have any particular task. Marija reports the Thursday message. During this period apparitions tend to last from four to seven minutes. Visionaries ask for the blessing of us all, of the sacred objects, but mainly for the sick. This is very important for all of you who come here to know that we receive Our Lady's blessing.

In the last message, given on the feast of the Assumption, Our Lady has invited us to live the message and has blessed us with a solemn blessing, allowed by the Lord.

So, even though She does not have a message for us every night, a message, nevertheless, does take place – Our Lady comes, She greets us through the visionaries, blesses us, leads us.

This is the fundamental message – Her special presence through which all else can be explained. This event has been lasting already fifty months and more and more people come, more and more books and films are being made on the subject.

This can only be explained because of Our Lady's presence. Also the healings, the new spirit of prayer, the spirit of fasting, of faith can only be explained by Her special presence, through which we receive graces, shall we say, in advance.

At this point it would be honest of us to wonder : « Why does Our Lady come, what does She want from us? ». She once said in a message, *« When the Lord comes, He does not come for fun.*

He comes in earnest ». Also in last Thursday's message to Mirjana.
She said, « *I have been calling you to conversion for the last four
years. This is something serious, be converted before it may be
too late* ». What does Our Lady want?

On the third day of the apparitions, Marija Pavlović told us she
had an apparition which remained engraved in her heart – she saw
Our Lady with a big cross and saying, « *Be reconciled, be recon-
ciled, be reconciled* », and told us Her name, « *I am the Queen of
Peace* ». She wants peace for us all. But what does peace mean?
Our Lady starts from our heart – peace in our heart, reconciliation
between us and God, between us and other men, forgiveness.
And She wants to teach us a new way to peace.

So look here, I ask myself – who to-day in this world can invite men
to peace? If a diplomat, a president, a political party does so,
others wonder what he really thinks. Words have lost their strength;
we no longer believe the words of those who say: « We want this »;
above all, when peace is at stake. Then the burden of politics and
diplomacy hangs over our words – here the visionaries have been
repeating for fifty months, without politics or diplomacy – « peace,
reconciliation ». And these events have led exactly to this. By
working together with the pilgrims, with the people who come
here, I am growing more and more in the belief of the goodness
of man. I have never met anybody here who does not want peace,
who does not want reconciliation and does not want to be loved
or to love. We carry within ourselves this very desire for peace,
but I also realise that we are very complicated; sin has ruined us.
Thus, Our Lady, through the visionaries – who have become simple
witnesses – wants us to get a move on.

But in order to have peace one must have faith, one must pray
and fast. And for faith, a few very simple facts are needed – look,
when the visionaries say, « We see Our Lady. We hear Her, we
speak to Her, we can hold Her by the hand, we can touch Her.
We have seen Paradise, Purgatory, Hell ». And when Ivanka says,
« I have seen my mother », all these facts are for us, for our faith.
We can once more sense that the hereafter does exist. The visionaries cannot produce theories on these matters. They say,

« we see » and that is all, without many explanations, as to how or why. They say, « we see; Our Lady is calling us ». And I tell you our faith is very superficial. All those who say, « I believe », perhaps only mean this: « I know that God exists », but faith means quite something else, a total abandonment to God. This is the faith Our Lady wants here – that we abandon ourselves and allow ourselves to be led.

In a message She said, « *I want to guide you, but you do not allow yourselves to be guided* ». So, what we are asked of is faith lived as abandonment, prayer and fasting.

In practical terms, everyday – the Creed, seven Our Father's, Hail Mary's, Glory Be's, the whole Rosary, the reading of the Bible and fasting twice weekly, confession once a month. When we start to do this, all else will be given to us. In the message of two or three weeks ago, Our Lady said, « *God wants to act through you. Open yourselves up. The Lord wants to give you what is necessary* ». Therefore, if we carry on praying, fasting and believing – obviously also with the grace of love – we will obtain all the rest. Peace and everything else will be granted as a grace, since Jesus was talking a great deal of this very peace when He said, « *The peace I give you the world cannot give* ». Money cannot give it to you, nor anything or anybody in this world.

The Rosary: perhaps someone wonders why one hundred and fifty Hail Mary's. I will tell you, it is very simple. This is a call to a form of prayer which is very suitable to the present time, repetitive, meditative, biblical and when you start praying the Rosary with all your heart, then you start learning from Our Lady how one should behave in this life, accepting the Lord's will – the way Our Lady does in the Annunciation or when visiting her cousin Elizabeth – thinking of others. Then prayer becomes a means by which to live with the Lord, to live with Our Lady, enabling us to learn about Christian life. Why must we learn about Christian life – we must and are under obligation to do so because we are Christians. The world is awaiting this help from us, it is looking for peace, for reconciliation. Sometimes we Christians live just like atheists, with no difference in our lives from those who say, « God does not exist ». We need a deeper conversion.

Our Lady wants us to abandon ourselves totally to the Lord, our hearts to belong to the Lord, so that we may lose nothing and receive everything. This is the same as when Our Lady invited us to pray the Creed at the beginning. "I believe" means to « give with one's heart », to entrust oneself to Someone, to give oneself up to Someone. All these events require us to give ourselves up totally, for us to give our hand to Our Lady, the Mother who calls us to peace each day.

(Fr. Slavko Barbarić - 22 August 1985)

« Engage yourselves in the fight against satan »

The focal point of this period can be summed up in two words – It is a period when Our Lady requires urgent conversion from us. On the other hand, Our Lady warns us about the presence of satan who is fighting against Her. To explain this better, I shall read to you the message Mirjana received on 15 August for the day of the Assumption and, in order to understand this message, I shall give you an introduction.

When Mirjana, back in June 1985, again met Our Lady, she informed us of the content of this meeting. During the meeting she received an order from Our Lady to inform a local priest of the first admonition to the world. The priest will come to know of it ten days beforehand and will have to be spiritually prepared to announce it to the world three days before it happens.

We asked the visionary, « Why does Our Lady appear to you more frequently now than before? ». The visionary replied by saying that Our Lady wants everything to proceed properly, with no mistakes, since – says the visionary – everything is heading towards the end: matters, future events are approaching.

When we asked the question, « And how do you feel now, with the young people in town? » she replied, « If God did not help me in a particular way. I would go mad ». « But why? ». She replied, « Because I know what will happen in the world and men continue to behave as if God did not exist ».

Now you will better understand the message of the 15 August: « *My Angel, pray for the unbeliever, people will tear their hair out. Brother will implore brother, he will curse his past life without God, will regret it, but it will be too late. After four years of my admonitions, now it is time for conversion. Pray for them* ». This message tells us for the umpteenth time that we must accept Our Lady in earnest, as She said through Jelena in the summer of 1983, *« Accept me in earnest – when God comes amongst you, He does not come for fun, but to say important things »*.

This word which we have heard through Mirjana brings us face to face with the apparitions, so that we must be really serious about Our Lady's messages and welcome them in earnest and bring them to others.

On the other hand, as I was saying to you, the distinguishing nature of the messages in the period July-August 1985, is one of constant struggle between Our Lady on one hand and satan on the other. When I talk to you of this reality, I talk because we have received the messages through the visionaries, and also because we have experienced those messages; we really have experienced these messages to be true.

At the beginning of July Our Lady gave the parish a message to pray more in order to banish satan from the parish and from all the pilgrims.

Afterwards, another message followed. She asked us to have the sacred objects blessed, to carry them on us, to place them in our families, in our homes, as a protection against satan.

It is typical of Blessed Mary to carry on urging us to pray and fight against satan.

The message of 8 August was very short. Our Lady was urging us to engage in the fight against satan: *« Now that you are aware of his action, he acts more aggressively. Therefore, take up your arms and with the Rosary in your hands, defeat him »*.

It is, in fact, the last message before the Assumption, in which Our Lady has invited us to engage in the fight against satan. And you know that when one enters into battle, one forgets everything – one's wife and husband, one's family and everyone – one must fight.

Therefore, one has to grasp this urgency on the part of Our Lady who, in Her message says, *« Engage yourselves in the fight against satan »*.

The last message is the following, « *To-day I would like to tell you that the Lord wants to put you to the test, which is something you can overcome with prayer. God tests you through your every day work. Now pray that you may overcome each one of these tests with calm. Through all these difficulties the Lord gives you, you open yourselves more to God every day and go towards Him with love. I thank you for responding to my call* ».

The characteristic of a vision Jelena had on 4 August will explain to us what we must do.

As the visionaries were getting ready for 5 August – and the visionaries say Our Lady told them that Her birthday falls on that very day – satan appeared to Jelena crying. He was telling the visionary, « Tell Her – that is Our Lady, because satan does not pronounce the name of Our Lady; nor the name of Our Lord – not to bless the world, at least not to-night ». And satan carried on crying. Our Lady appeared immediately and blessed the world. Satan fled at once. Our Lady said, « *I know him only too well, he has escaped, but will soon be back tempting people* ».

In Our Lady's blessing of that evening there was the guarantee – as the visionary told us – that the following day 5 August satan could not have been able to tempt anyone. There, you see the strength of the blessing. You can therefore understand the message of 15 August, passed on through the visionary Marija, when Our Lady gave us a solemn blessing, since God has charged Her to give people the solemn blessing.

The greatest thing Our Lady could give us was the solemn blessing. In fact, those who were present during these two days (5 and 15 August) experienced a particular grace in their hearts.

Now, on our part, it is not enough to listen to the messages, but it is important to accept them. And, during this period, to really live conversion and invite everyone to conversion and announce the need for conversion to all men.

Moreover, our task is to pray a lot, so that the blessing of God and the blessing of Our Lady may descend upon us, so that the blessing may drive satan away from us.

In my opinion many pilgrims remain somnolent after hearing these words and do nothing or little about it. What is needed, is for each one of us, on hearing these words, to be moved to pray more, to do penance and to be witnesses of the messages.

Indeed, in to-day's liturgy we have been asked whether we want to follow Jesus or be taken away from Him. When dealing with the announcement of the message of today's Gospel, we must really concentrate on what has happened during these last four Sundays, as we are following the very chapter of the Gospel of St. John (Ch. 6).

In the beginning, many, many people followed Jesus. Then when Jesus was wanting to enter into the full depth of Christian life, of the life of the believers, people began wandering away, even some of his disciples wandered off. And finally Jesus told the Twelve, « Have you also decided to forsake me? ». So Peter said, « No Lord, you alone have words of eternal life ».

At the very moment of answering to Jesus' calls we must do it in a practical way; by entering more and more deeply into the Christian life and into the Gospel.

These words sent to us by Our Lady are a wish from God – that each one of us be converted, that we answer with our own life, in a realistic way, to what we hear in the Church and also what we hear through the Blessed Virgin. I think Our Lady's messages are quite serious, the very ones you heard this evening. Place them in your hearts and answer in a practical way, in order to make a deep confession. Confession will then be the start or the continuation of conversion. After which, take up these messages Our Lady has given us for the last four years.

Remember – at the beginning Our Lady invited everyone to pray every day, a minimum of seven Our Father's, Hail Mary's, Glory Be's and one Creed. She then invited us to pray the whole Rosary every day, to go to monthly confession so as to be able to approach Communion, and fasting at least on a Friday on bread and water. Lastly, She invited us to fast one more day, on the Wednesday, so that the Holy Spirit may descend on the world.

Also you should put yourselves on the path of the messages. Do not say, « I have no time for prayer ». Put some order in your daily lives, make sure you also have times when you can be with God. Recently I was pleased to hear of the example set by the head of a family, here in Medjugorje, whose house is rather big and who puts pilgrims up for the night. At night, at ten oclock, he tells all the pilgrims, « You can stay as long as you want and talk quietly: I am now retiring with my family to pray. You can stay as long as you like, but to-morrow you will all be up at six to start your prayers. Those who wish to live in my house will start their day with the prayer of the Rosary and the other prayers ».

You too, try and follow this example, set a time in your families, in your life when meeting with God can also take place.

(Fr. Tomislav Vlašić - 25 August 1985)

Our Lady makes us responsible for peace in this world

Our Lady tells Mirjana a lot about unbelievers and always invites her to pray for them.

Everyday we get closer to the end of the apparitions and to the events predicted in the messages, but we do not know when and how this will happen. Our Lady invites us all to reconciliation and peace in the whole world. In a message She said that with prayer and fasting one can even dispel wars. I am telling you that Our Lady makes us responsible for peace in this world, and we are invited to allow ourselves to be made responsible. None of us can then say, « What can I do? I am not a diplomat, I am not a politician... ».

Our Lady makes us responsible and perhaps we can even say that if there are wars in this world, or if wars threaten us, we are already responsible. In fact, if there are still wars and Our Lady says, « *They can be prevented by prayer and fasting* », we have not fasted or prayed enough.

And just look at a very important similarity, also in the sense of responsability for peace – seventeen years after the beginning of this century, Our Lady appears in Fatima and to-day, at the end of the century, in Medjugorje.

This similarity also makes us think, so that we may not look for easy excuses not to pray or fast. And here we must discern one thing – many people, even amongst priests and bishops, do not discern the difference between the recognition of the apparitions on the part of the Church and the message.

If someone is waiting for recognition by the Church, he is doing so together with us – I too am waiting for it. But if someone is waiting for the recognition from the Church of the message, of prayer for peace, of fasting for peace, on reconciliation, he is not doing the right thing, for we know the message and it is already given in the Bible.

So, at the present moment we can look at the message and see that we need peace. Who says we do not need it? We can plainly see that there is a need for it. Consider the fact that Our Lady has not appeared in order to fight for Her own recognition within the Church; She has already been recognised. When She pronounced Her name, She did not say, « I am Our Lady, who is looking for Her recognition ». She said, « *I am the Queen of Peace* ». « *Be reconciled* ». And here we must stop and make a distinction between things – each one of us who has started fasting, praying, being reconciled, is doing well, surely, even though he is waiting for the official recognition of the Church.

But faith is something else.

Just think that the first prayer She asked for was the Creed. The Creed means « To give with one's heart », to abandon oneself to the Lord, to believe.

I can honestly say that one of my deepest experiences is the following: our faith is a superficial one, totally superficial.

I can see many people thinking, when saying, « I Believe », « I know a God does exist », but if this God has a say, if He has a right to speak in my life, then it is not enough to know that God exists; in the same way it is not enough for a little boy who is crying, to say that a father and a mother exist. The little boy will again become calm only when he finds himself in his mother's or father's arms. In the same way, faith means abandonment, letting the Lord guide you. Look at it this way, every distressing worry, every attachment to this world, every selfishness, every excuse for not having forgiven, is a sign for us that our faith is superficial. If our faith were deeper, if for us, it meant an abandonment to the Lord, then we should have no trouble in forgiving, in sharing, in thinking of others, in loving. Obviously, all those who accept these facts have started praying and fasting. As far as prayer is concerned, Our Lady is asking for the Creed and seven Our Father's, the whole Rosary, everyday.

This is how we pray in church every evening.

Our Lady is not asking for the formula of the apostolic Creed. but She is asking for a decision for the Lord and I believe that for this very reason She has asked us to meditate on the passage of the Gospel, Matthew 6,24-34, where it says that one cannot serve two masters. She is asking for a decision. Why should there be distressing worries? The Father knows everything about you and He loves you – « Seek, first of all the Kingdom of God ». We meditate on this evangelical passage every Thursday during adoration.

Why the Rosary? The Rosary is a biblical, meditative, repetitive prayer, a very simple one, suitable for prayer in families, where there are also children.

It must really become the prayer of the heart. The meaning of the Rosary is to be together, to live together with Our Lady and Jesus, learning from them the love for our neighbour, the bearing of sorrows, or our crosses. One could pray in families – if you cannot say the three parts, pray together one part of the Rosary and the remaining two on your own.

Our Lady asked for active prayer. You will understand what that means if you listen carefully to this question: « Who is active in your family, as far as prayer goes? ». I shall make myself clear. Who says, « Let us now switch off the TV, the radio, the telephone. for now we must pray? ». Who is it in your family who says, « Today I have had a conflict, it will do us good to meditate on this passage of the Gospel »? Or, if we have had a joy, who looks for another passage of the Gospel which might help us? Now, who is it who does this? I know of a head of a family who tells his family members, « You will read the prayer to-morrow », and to another, « you the day after », and in this way, every member becomes active. If a family is united in prayer, it will understand what praying means.

A pilgrim told me of his experience: « I started to pray the Rosary in the car and noticed that I was absent-minded. Should I carry on or not? ». I told him, « Certainly, it is far better to pray a distracted Rosary than to swear at others when you drive your car ». Pray, no matter how!

Our Lady is not asking for one hundred and fifty Hail Marys; if someone thinks that way he will not be able to pray for much longer or, if he does, he will say, « I have finished for to-day, to-morrow I must pray again ». Our Lady is asking for prayer as a means of obtaining peace, joy, of overcoming the tiredness of the soul, the spiritual tiredness, of overcoming difficult situations. She is also asking for fasting. Why and how? There is a very simple answer to that. The ideal one is on bread and water for two days, on Wednesdays and Fridays; if someone cannot live on bread and water, let him fast the best way he can, in any case food must be restricted to the absolute minimum.

Our Lady wants us to fast. Fasting as a way of ridding ourselves of the material world, well and truly detaching ourselves from it. If you draw near to the wall of your house, really close, you do not see anybody in your household; even if your best friends are there, you will not see them. You will not see anything. But if you take a few steps back, you will see the house and all that is happening in it.

Many people in this world have become just like that – more and more money, owning more and more. Thus we have become blind, and wars come, not because we share, but because we want to take from others.

For this reason Our Lady says « *Fast* » – not to make us die, but to show us how one becomes free.

This interior freedom is for the Lord and for others. This fasting also has an Eucharistic dimension – if we fast we have discovered bread, and more easily shall we also discover the Eucharistic bread.

(Fr. Slavko Barbarić - 4 September 1985)

Here heaven is speaking

Every Thursday, Our Lady is giving messages through Marija Pavlović. On the one hand these messages describe our present situation whilst, on the other hand, they are an impulse to go further and further ahead in prayer, in fasting, in our abandonment to God – a letting ourselves be guided by the Lord.

Last Thursday's message is very simple, but also very deep, « *I am inviting you once more to prayer. Satan now wants to use the grapes of your vineyard for his purpose. Pray that he may not succeed* ». What does this mean? Look, the vineyard is one word or one parable of the Gospel. Our Lady talks biblically.

So many times one reads in the Psalms of how the Lord has planted a vineyard, or how He wants to keep it... On the other hand Our Lady is a good teacher – She borrows images and symbols from everyday life. Now it is the vineyards. She is using the grapes of the vineyards as a symbol for any form of materialism.

Your vineyard or your grapes in the vineyard, even though you may live in town and only see it on television, could be your money, something bothering you so much that you are not able to pray or be reconciled or forgive.

A third consideration, strictly in basic terms, which we often preach from the altar about is this: there are people – even around here – who, having noticed the flow of foreign pilgrims, are selling grapes at an incredible price, much too high, much higher than they are worth.

So this is a test, a temptation for those who are attached to money, who want to earn. Therefore, Our Lady wants to educate us at different levels and tell us to « pay attention », because any attachment to materialism of any sort is a danger to man, to faith, to love, to reconciliation, also to peace, since wars come because we want to take from others...

... I can tell you of my experiences here – I have been here forty months now and I do not know how much longer I shall still be here. I see us receiving a grace in advance here. There are many people coming here who are ready to pray, fast, be reconciled, confess; really wonderful conversions. And this has not been going on for one month or a fortnight, but for fifty-one months. Everyday, this is for me, a new proof to see that Our Lord is present in a special way and that He is inviting us through Our Lady.

Who can possibly, at this time, invite us to peace in the world?

If a politician does so, people do not believe his words and say, « Maybe it is sheer diplomacy ». If someone else says so – it is the same again.

Here the visionaries convey messages, they convey them to us and say, « Be reconciled, peace », and more and more people come from all over the world.

At four o'clock I was speaking to a group of people coming from Egypt. In these days there is a book being published in Arabic in Egypt. Already there are some booklets in Chinese, too.

I seem to be able to explain it this way – here Heaven is speaking. Yet again, it is the word without politics or diplomacy which can find its direct path to our heart. I know many people having already come once, tend to come again. This is quite inexplicable to me, since anybody can see that we do not have good parking spaces, we still do not have proper facilities, we do not have good homes to lodge people or good hotels.

But I can see that, all of a sudden, when essential things are at stake, all this becomes a question of secondary importance.

Then Heaven surely is speaking and inviting us. I can honestly say that many people in the world, millions of people are now fasting, praying for peace, getting ready to be reconciled.

(Fr. Slavko Barbarić - 5 September 1985)

The fight between Our Lady and satan is a supernatural fight and supernatural means are needed

You know the news already. I would rather like to place a few words and a few facts about Medjugorje inside your hearts so that you may live the reality of Medjugorje.

By taking a look at all the messages of the last two months, one thing appears clear – one can see the Woman clad in sun fighting against satan. It is very important to see this in order to recognise Our Lady in Medjugorje. Moreover, it is very important to understand why God is telling us these things through Our Lady.

In my opinion, we should first of all try to understand our duty in this struggle in which we are now living and understand the means with which we can fight against satan.

The message that has mostly been engraved in my heart in the last few months has been the one of 8 August, when Our Lady told us, « *Engage yourselves in the fight against satan* ».

When one goes to war, one forgets everything, one forsakes everything. Our religious attitude at the moment should be the one of engagement in fight – as Our Lady says – in order to defeat him. The other phrase Our Lady said in the same message is, « *When you are more aware of satan's action, he acts more strongly* ».

What we are dealing with here are the messages of Our Lady in Medjugorje, not news in the press, we are not dealing with a theory. For us who have lived and still live here, the messages are a revelation, in the sense that we discover the reality of faith, the warnings of Our Lady being just the arrows which make us discover the presence of satan. Unfortunately, much has been debated amongst priests and theologians on the existence of satan, and there are many to-day who actually deny it. In Medjugorje we have seen him, met him, we have experienced his presence, we have come to know him and the means with which to defeat him. Every message of Our Lady was a warning about what would then happen, so by putting into practice the very things Our Lady was telling us, we have discovered his presence.

I have just been saying that we have discovered his presence – people and priests have felt satan's action in different ways. For instance, during Mass, when they have been attacked in an incredible way – they were unable to be recollected, they had really some horrible thoughts against Jesus, against the Eucharist; they then had several attacks against their families and attacks against priests. All this we have experienced for ourselves.

Especially these last few months, we have had some people becoming obsessed. We may have experienced satan's attacks, but we have, at the same time, experienced ways of defeating him.

In the same message of 8 August, Our Lady said, « *Take up your arms and with the Rosary in your hands, defeat him* ».

We have learned that one cannot fight the evil of the world with human reasoning, with scientific reasoning, not even with Bible studies or with theological studies, but with one's faith, one's love, one's prayer.

The fight between Our Lady and satan is a supernatural fight and supernatural means are needed.

If I look at the messages, in all of them Our Lady makes an appeal, « *Pray in order to defeat him, in order to gain victory over him* ». And at this very moment we must remind ourselves of all the messages Our Lady was saying from the beginning, « *Peace of heart, prayer, fasting, conversion* ».

This is the path of Our Lady's strategy and we must follow Her. When satan's temptations are present, I am also telling you pilgrims, « Be careful not to accept his poison ». Satan is a muddler; he is a deceiving being; do not allow confusion inside your hearts – many pilgrims live in some sort of confusion with so many inner questions: « Some people say this, some say... the Church has not pronounced herself yet... I do not know how to go about it... ». Do not allow this confusion to reign. If you have your questions and your doubts, then do what Our Lady did. Our Lady herself had doubts when the Angel presented himself to Her, « How can it be? How can I conceive without a husband? ».

Indeed She asked God questions such as – « God enlighten my mind. How can I? ». If you have doubts go to God, so that God may solve your doubts, so that God may give you light, and God will give you light.

Please do not live in confusion, since confusion comes from satan, since confusion holds us back, it does not allow us to walk, to go ahead. Go ahead.

Many say the Church has not defined her position yet. But this does not matter, it is of no account. We must understand the role of the hierarchy – it is waiting, it is waiting for us to grow, for us to become holy, so that one day the Church may say that these people are really saintly and that all this really comes from God.

She is waiting for us to walk just as a mother waits for her child to walk. But we must not wait for the final pronouncement of the Church, for the Church to confirm all this. We must grow spiritually. That is why I am telling you – « Do not live in confusion » – tell others as well; to those who ask you questions, announce the word of God and the word of Our Lady, bring light.

When I am asking you not to live in confusion, I am asking you to walk on facts. Never, in the whole history of the Church, have apparitions been so scientifically described, as with us in Medjugorje. By now you also have films and even a scientific book on what is happening during the ecstasy.

It is a fact. Experts say it is a fact, that the ecstasy is a fact. We are therefore facing a fact about which there is no question and we know of that very fact only through the visionaries who say, « Our Lady has appeared and is appearing to mankind for the last time. She has come to tell us of important and urgent matters – peace, conversion, fasting and prayer ».

And this matter which the visionaries express is something which cannot be discussed otherwise; if we start discussing this, then we Christians have started arguing about our own name, since the only way leading us to sanctification is prayer, fasting, conversion.

And there is another fact that we must welcome – here in Medjugorje we have seen other phenomena – you may have done as well – which confirm the so-called signs in heaven and on earth. We priests have seen other facts – the deepest conversion of people. I cannot easily forget, for instance, the day of St. James: in the evening I had been hearing confession for three hours, mostly Italians. One quarter of the people had not been to confession for decades. They come here looking for God.

These are not facts you skip over and forget, they are to be accepted. People's faces as well, if you have noticed – they speak for themselves, they are a fact. People there are not thinking so much of Our Lady as of what Our Lady has given birth to here in Medjugorje – a new life and people have experienced this new life. When you ask people, « Do you believe in the apparitions? ». They say, « No, I know it », because people know it. Not only do they believe, but they know it because they have experienced a new life.

There is only one more fact to be borne in mind – it is only through prayer, fasting and conversion that we will come to a supernatural understanding of the news. Therefore, I ask you to follow Our Lady's messages through a deepening of your prayer.

I am telling you in all honesty, that four years of apparitions are a teaching for the deepening of one's prayer. It is not books, but the simple stimuli on the part of Our Lady that urged us ahead, and each stimulus was for us a ray, telling us how to deepen our path. Pray much individually, pray also much in your families.

(Fr. Tomislav Vlašić - 6 September 1985)

« Pray for the fulfilment of all that God is planning for this parish »

I shall read out and explain yesterday's message. « *Dear children, I am thanking you to-day for all your prayers. Pray even more, so that satan will be driven away from this place. Dear children, satan's plan has failed. Pray for the fulfilment of all that God is planning in this parish. I thank the youth here most especially, for the sacrifices they have offered. Thank you for responding to my call* ».

In these words one can feel the Mother, the Mother who is always hoping that Her children will do well. A Mother – I would say – who is optimistic even when saying, « You have not done well, or you have forgotten » and then, at the end, saying, « *Thank you for listening, for having responded to my call* ».

A theologian who was here, when he heard these things for the first time said, « In the text Our Lady reprimands us, then She says, "*I thank you for responding to my call*": it is impossible, Father, this is a contradiction ». I replied, « Be careful, in the words of a mother you can always find contradictions. The moment she reproaches, she also invites and gives at the same time ». On a pedagogical level one can say – there is no contradiction. Obviously one could argue – how can one thank and say, « You have not responded? ». But She wants to educate us. And this, it seems to me, is a very important thing. Our Lady is showing herself to be a Mother, a friend of the visionaries. They meet, they talk, they touch Her, they see Her in three dimensions. She leads them and through them She leads us.

She is close. One loses one's fears. She is here and we have become used to it.

This is the structure of the messages where Our Lady shows herself as Mother, as Teacher, as someone who knows how to talk, and by talking, how to educate. In these messages She thanks people for all their prayers. It is nice to hear that. I do not know who has been praying – anyway Our Lady sees, hears and thanks.

And from this point of view, we must look again and even wonder how – according to this message – She thanks our hearts with this « thank you ». But if in my heart, your heart, there is still resentment, if there is anguish, if there is fear or something else, perhaps we have become blind with all that we have, that has been given to us as a gift...

Therefore, if Our Lady thanks us, we really have to ask ourselves – does our heart know how to thank? If it does not, especially if someone says, « To thank, what for? » it is a true sign that we have become blind.

But look how the Mother says, « *Thank you* » and, at the same time: « *Pray even more* ».

Just like a mother saying to her son, « You have been very good to-day », and at the same time she says, « I hope, however, that tomorrow you will be better still ».

Our Lady does the same. Then we must pray even more when She says, « *So that satan may be driven away from this place* ».

Judging by all messages, mainly of July and August of this year, it seems to me that in every message She has spoken of satan as someone who wants to destroy, who wants to hurt us, who wants to take away from us peace or reconciliation.

In a message of August, I believe, She said, « *Pray that you may hear my call* » and beware, satan wants to stop it. I am saying this and repeating this for your own benefit – it seems to me that satan's primary task is to stop us from hearing the call, because Our Lady has the word ready for us, for our consolation, for our healing, for our comfort. But if satan succeeds in preventing us from hearing these words, we stay where we are and do not move on. If satan, in fact, prevents us from listening to these events of Medjugorje, then he has stopped many a ear from hearing the message.

For example, how many people have been thinking or still are thinking today of hallucinations? Of all those who have come here, of all the doctors, psychologists, psychiatrists, none of them has stated that they are hallucinations. Only those living far away from us say this.

I ask you to be careful when you hear the message. If you have any problems in your life, perhaps you will ask yourself, « Where is the Lord, why has He forsaken me? ». This does not come from the good Spirit, it is certainly not coming from the Holy Spirit who counsels us. It is coming from another spirit. If we bear resentment in our hearts, if we say, « I do not wish to be reconciled, I do not wish to forgive because I am offended », I am telling you to beware because these things do not come from a good spirit. Therefore, Our Lady says, « *Pray that he may be driven away* ».

It is very important that he should be far away from this place, because here Our Lord is speaking and He wants to find our hearts and move us onwards. And the one thing that gives us hope is when She says, « *Dear children. Satan's plan has failed* ».

We hope and know that Our Lord has won. The Kingdom of the Lord is the kingdom of peace, love, of reconciliation. The Lord Jesus has conquered the kingdom of satan with His Cross. But satan still remains active.

We were told the same thing by Jelena, yesterday. Our Lady was full of joy and said, « *Satan's plan has failed* ». But Jelena said that towards the end of the vision Our Lady's face had once again become serious and She said, « *Beware, satan will not abandon the fight* ». Obviously this is quite clear.

But in January Our Lady said that, with fervent prayer and love, one can disarm him with no difficulty at all. I shall explain the last message a little and you shall see how much there is to be said. Yet another appeal – pray for the fulfilment of all God is planning in this parish. We do not know what the Lord is planning but, according to what has been expressed by the visonaries, it is something great. Not just for this parish, but for the whole world. For instance, a great sign and other things which we shall see, have been announced. Surely a great plan.

I had a talk with Jelena this afternoon, Jelena being the girl who receives the locutio interna; she receives various visions and she

82

was telling me that in one vision she saw satan offering Our Lord all his kingdom in order to win here in Medjugorje.

Is that clear to you? Satan is, therefore, offering the Lord all the other kingdom to hinder fulfilment of the plans.

I asked her, « Jelena, how is that? ». « Look – she replied – the way I understood it is this – many have received a new hope in Medjugorje. If satan were to succeed in destroying this plan, everyone, or at least many, would lose this hope ».

According to the theologians and the priests, if someone wonders, « How can Our Lord deal with satan like this, or satan with Our Lord? ». This is certainly a biblical account. In the book of Job we also find similar things, in which satan facing the Lord's throne says, « Give me Job, your servant and I shall show you that he will not be faithful to you ». And then the Lord told satan to test him.

Ultimately, this is true: satan fights against peace, against love, against reconciliation with all possible means and if Our Lady did say in a message, « *Satan has now become stronger and acts in a stronger way because we have discovered him* », this is also very important to know. Anyone who has been in the army will know that the best tactic is if the enemy on the other side starts thinking that the others do not want to fight, because then they let temselves go.

She said, « *We have discovered him and now he is getting a lot stronger, he is getting angry...* ».

So we just do not know what the Lord is planning for this Parish and for the whole world.

After fifty one months from the first apparition one can see the urgency of conversion, of faith and also of peace. One can also see that Our Lord has a great plan. We have seen that whenever in trouble, Medjugorje has always received fresh impulse and help, even from men themselves.

One can therefore see that Our Lord guides us through all the troubles, through all trials. But He can only guide us if He has found – and still finds – people who listen to Him, people who pray, people who fast. And so it is very important to see how each one of us who takes up prayer and fasting, by so doing helps the Lord, and at the same time, helps himself as well.

Because everything that God plans through Our Mother can only be for our own good. Our Lady then especially thanks the youth for the sacrifices they have offered. I do not know who, at this moment in time, is feeling young and hears this word « thank you » and is accepting it as if addressed to himself; in any case I can say two things – many young people of this Parish and of the entire world certainly pray a lot and make sacrifices. If Our Lady is thanking the youth, I really think She is addressing Herself to the young of age...

This is very important. Who is young? Young is he who is open, who allows himself to be moved on, who says, « I can, I will try, I want to start again ». If you are 60, 70 or 90 say, « I want to start afresh », then you are young.

And if a youngster of 20 says, « I cannot take it any more, I cannot find any sense in my life, I do not want to study... » he is old, even though he is 20.

So surely, when Our Lady says, « *I thank the youth* », She is thanking all those who have replied in prayer, in fasting and in faith, those who have allowed themselves to be made responsible for peace in the world.

(Fr. Slavko Barbarić - 6 September 1985)

We are all invited to peace and reconciliation

Welcome everybody. You are with us because you believe in the testimony of our visionaries.

We are now in the fifty-first month, since they started being witnesses to seeing Our Lady.

I have just come from a long chat with the doctors. Even in Zagreb (they are all psychiatrists and psychologists) the last word was, « This phenomenon is highly complicated for us. It is very difficult to explain. A great many aspects have to be taken into account in order to see what it is all about ».

For the visionaries, however, it is very simple, from the start until now they say: « We see Our Lady. We see Her in three dimensions. the same way we see one another. We can talk to Her, we pray with Her, we can hear Her, we see Her clearly, we can touch Her ».

Our Lady is giving us messages, She is inviting us to prayer, peace, reconciliation, faith and fasting, and it cannot be any other way. Faith and spirituality are something quite other than medicine. psychology...

Why does this happen? It happens for one reason only. We are all invited to peace and reconciliation. And we are all in great need of this very peace – individuals, families, the Church and the whole world. According to all these messages – one could say – Our Lady is making us responsible for peace. And I do believe Our Lady knows what She is doing, what She is saying – namely, that we must allow ourselves to be made responsible.

Please do not wash your hands of it by saying, « I am not a diplomat, I am not a politician, peace does not depend on me ».

Peace depends on us all.

This, it seems to me, is the most important thing – to look with a new heart, with a new eye at one's own responsibility in this world and at all that is going on around us. How can we give our personal response to all this which we are invited to?

Our Lady said, « *Pray and Fast* ».

This we must do in order to obtain peace in our hearts and to enable us to bring peace to others.

This is perhaps the hardest way to obtain peace, but is it not perhaps the only one?

Conversion is asked of us all – a change in one's own everyday life. And this is the most difficult thing of all.

Sometimes it is easier to give money to the poor than to forgive someone for a word or to forget an insult. But it is only on these grounds that one can build up peace: by being reconciled and by forgiving.

And every man who is reconciled, every family who lives in peace is always a new sign that peace is possible and, with each reconciled person, the entire world is brought closer to peace.

(Fr. Slavko Barbarić - 7 September 1985)

The kind of faith Our Lady wants us to learn about is abandonment to the Lord

We have just heard Dr. Frigerio of the medical team in Milan saying that where technology, science, medicine, psychology and psychiatry stop, faith must carry on. It is true – as Dr. Frigerio affirmed – and previously Dr. Joyeux, « We have found our limits, and can honestly say that it is not a question of illness or of a pathology. The visionaries are healthy in body and soul ». These positive encouragements do exist and now, for someone who believes, what is there left to do? Either one throws everything away and says he is not interested or one takes a dive into faith. And this is the very point from which everything happens. When the visionaries talk about this phenomenon, they speak very simply. « We start to pray, a glow appears, we kneel down, we begin to speak, we receive the messages, we touch Our Lady, we hear Her, we see Her, She shows us Paradise, Hell, Purgatory... ».

What they tell us is very simple indeed.

These encounters fill a person with joy and peace. When we start explaining with our own means, we come across words whose meaning we do not understand – there are many gadgets, many specialists pointing to a clue, others to some other clue. But thousands of clues do not make up proof. Now look, you either throw away everything or you accept what the visionaries say. And we are under moral obligation to believe a person who speaks the truth, until we find it to be false. Therefore, I can say at this point, « I have a duty and I believe in what the visionaries say ». I know that the simplicity of their affirmations is something given to us for the benefit of our faith.

The Lord does not want, through these phenomena, to show doctors that they still do not know so many things. No, He does not;

what He wants to tell us is – Look, you are looking at tangible signs and therefore you can believe, have trust in Me and let yourselves be guided. Through these simple facts, inexplicable to us, Our Lady wants that we, who live in a rational world, be once again able to open ourselves to the reality of the hereafter.

When I first spoke to Fr. Gobbi, he asked me what Our Lady is asking of the priests. I told him that there is no special message. Only once did She say that priests have to be faithful and preserve people's faith. This is the point which follows on from Fatima.

My deepest experience is the following – we are all very superficial in our faith.

The kind of faith Our Lady wants us to learn about is abandonment to the Lord, letting ourselves be guided by Our Lady who is still coming every evening.

So, at this stage, She has asked first of all for the Creed. « Giving with our hearts », abandoning ourselves. One can give one's heart to somebody one loves, to somebody one trusts. She is asking, amongst other things, for our weekly meditation of the passage of the Gospel, Matthew VI,24-34, where it says that one cannot serve two masters. Hence a decision.

And then She says, why worry, why grieve? The Father knows all. Seek first the kingdom of Heaven. This is also the message of faith.

Fasting is also very useful for our faith – one can more easily hear the voice of the Lord and can also understand more easily one's neighbour. It is a kind of faith which means – in my life, as in yours – abandonment.

By the same token, any distress, any distressing situation, any fear, every conflict is a sign of our hearts not yet knowing Our Father nor Our Mother.

It is not enough for a little boy who is crying to know that a father and a mother exist – he only quietens down, he only finds peace when he is in his father's or mother's arms.

The same goes for faith: one can only allow oneself to be led if one starts to pray, if one starts to fast. You will find excuses every day for not having time, until you have discovered the value of prayer. When you have finally discovered it, you will have a lot of time for prayer.

Any situation will be a new one, also for prayer. And I am telling you that we have become real champions in finding excuses when it comes to prayer and fasting, but Our Lady does not want to accept these excuses any longer.

(Fr. Slavko Barbarić - 8 September 1985)

It is God who triumphs over satan

The emphasis of the message for this period is the following: Our Lady has talked a lot about the fact of satan's presence. In almost every message Our Lady warns us of the reality of satan. For us who have followed closely these messages and the events of Medjugorje, these messages are warnings based on what we have been able to experience for ourselves, a real revelation of satan's presence. It has not been a revelation in the sense that it has added anything new, but rather a new discovery of satan's presence.

By what Our Lady told us and the way She has followed us, we learnt how to face satan's presence and how to fight against him. In order to explain this better – lately several possessed people have arrived in Medjugorje together with those who have consecrated themselves to satan, wishing to bring evil. As we have been able to experience for ourselves, they left because they were afraid to stay here without being able to do anything. Other possessed people were unable to even enter the church; they refused to do so with all their strength. Furthermore, we had a particular case of an Italian woman who came here at the beginning of August showing all the signs of possession, and when Fr. Slavko started exorcism according to the directions of the Church, the woman burst out saying, « Leave me alone. This prayer is tiring me out, do not pray. Do not pray this prayer ever again, it torments me, it tires me out ». Then, all of a sudden she let loose and attacked the Father.

Through the visionary Our Lady gave the Father a message not to stay on his own with the possessed woman as she had every intention to kill him.

Later the Father was able to prove all this to himself and the woman, on returning to a state of consciousness, actually admitted it to him. The community carried on praying for this person and after two weeks she confessed – she told her whole life story and freed herself.

Last year I experienced another such case, again to do with an Italian woman; it took about ten priests to pray and another five to hold her down, as she wanted to destroy every sacred object, and after one hour and a half she – not actually the woman herself, since she was not conscious of what she was doing – started saying, « Leave me alone, do not pray any more, your prayers burn me, I cannot stand you any longer ». Finally, she was freed and started invoking the name of Jesus, praising Him, and became full of joy, full of peace.

I have just presented you with these two experiences so that you may understand the warnings Our Lady was giving us, warnings, which we were soon afterwards to experience and live as real facts. We have actually experienced what Our Lady was telling us. For instance, on 16 July the young visionary Jelena saw satan all upset thinking, « I must do something against Medjugorje. I must turn away some of the members of the prayer group. I shall make a few morally tepid, I shall put into the minds of others several episodes of a certain film, so that during Mass they will be distracted and will later run home to watch TV. I shall give those at the TV studios plenty of money in order to produce more films, to detach people from prayer ».

According to the visionary, after that Our Lady appeared saying, « *Yes, satan abandoned many people in order to come here and tempt the people in Medjugorje. Priests, visionaries and members of the prayer group will be particular targets* ». We were to experience this afterwards. Some people during Mass have had some terrible distractions, some real attacks – they felt an urge to curse the Eucharist, could not recognise themselves and had to fight. So, I have told you this just to explain the message, because the messages we have followed are no theory, but something we have actually felt, we have actually experienced. On the other hand, we have also experienced the weapons Our Lady pointed out to us.

As I was saying earlier to the pilgrims, last spring Our Lady showed us how one can be protected, defended against satan and told us that humility, sincerity, powerful prayer, mutual love will not allow satan to come anywhere near us. To explain this better, one evening She gave the prayer group the following task, « *Tomorrow, try and do everything with love, even what you do not like, accept it with divine love* ». This small group followed this message and the following day, in the evening, Jelena reported Our Lady to have said, « *Dear children, if you only knew how satan ran away from you!* ».

So you see, where there is God's presence, where we really live in God, where the Gospel is within us, satan can go round us in circles, but never attack us. We have experienced it. If you look at the messages, in every message Our Lady says, « *Pray, with prayer you will be able to triumph over him* ».

In a message to priests She said, « *Devote some time to the Rosary, the Rosary will protect the Catholic Church from the evil that satan wants to inflict upon Her at this very moment in time. Priests, devote your time to the Rosary* ».

Just think, when She warns us of satan's presence, She always asks for prayer. We have actually experienced that one cannot fight against evil with human reasoning, with human logic, but only with the divine grace that comes through faith, through abandonment to God, through prayer.

Then it is God who triumphs over satan. We have come to realise that we must really be at Our Lady's disposal, by living our Christian reality just as God wants us to. What must I do, what must we do when Our Lady says, « *conversion and prayer?* ». In one message She says that prayer ought to be a moment of reflection, a moment that is to say, when you see everything clearly, when you learn to cry, when you learn to be happy. Thus, in prayer you are being changed.

The episode of an American convert now springs to my mind – how he described the moment when he started witnessing to others. What happened is this – He had been stabbed, taken to hospital and was due to come out the following day. « In the evening – he says – they brought an old man into my room, he seemed to be asleep, so I knelt by my bed and started talking aloud to my God, as I felt this need, and started asking Him to forgive my friend Joe who had misunderstood me, who had offended me. I prayed that he may know Jesus Christ, then I prayed for the girl who was a cause of temptation. I then forgave the nurse who I had been hard on; I then said, O lord, I am ready to die for You. Give me strength and life, that I may go to my parents and announce Jesus Christ ». This man then said, « I remained in prayer with my God for a long time ».

As I got up in the morning, ready to leave the room, that old man made a sign to me to come nearer; he had a probe fitted and said in a low tone of voice, « Thank you, your prayer has saved me ». « But I was not praying for you » I said. « No, you are wrong – said the old man – you have prayed for me and, after so many years, last night I got down to praying again myself. I too offered my life to Jesus Christ. For me, this episode was the beginning of a testimony ». I brought this experience to your attention only to prove that one's life becomes saved through the grace of Jesus Christ.

If, by living, I can be a witness to all those around me, then I can carry the voice of God, I can carry His messages. If I do not live the Gospel in a radical way, I cannot even bring my testimony to others. Therefore, I would like to ask you pilgrims to live this reality through prayer, because prayer is a reality which renews itself daily. Each daily encounter with Our Lord brings something new and the dimension of prayer itself becomes new, so, if I say to you, « Prayer », this is really too little, I would rather say to you, « start praying, carry on praying, deepen your prayer ».

Lately, a small group, part of the prayer group, confided in me by saying that Our Lady has instructed them, through the visionary, to go to bed every night like this – kneeling in front of the cross, pray five mysteries of the Rosary of Jesus Christ. After the fifth mystery one should go to bed and carry on praying the other mysteries in order to stay with the Father, since the human spirit is lost even during the night, if one is not in God.

To end the day in God in this way and to continue with God on the next day. So when I want to talk to you about prayer, I want to tell you the messages that bring us to this reality: to come to God, to stay with God and to live with God.

Remember that in other previous messages Our Lady was asking not only for seven Our Father's, Hail Mary's, Glory Be's and the Rosary, but She was making us put the Our Father into practice, in such a way that we could live every word of it. She was instructing us to meditate on the Gospel, on how to live the Gospel all day. I can only say to you, « Put yourselves at God's disposal, take the Gospel seriously and you will understand everything ». The divine grace will follow each one of us if we put ourselves at God's disposal.

And now I give you my blessing:

By the intercession of the Blessed Virgin Mary Queen of Peace, may the Lord enlighten you, give you strength of body and soul, may the lord heal first of all your souls, so that each of you may seek first of all the Kingdom of God and trust to be granted everything else; may the Lord finally transform your lives into the real living Gospel.

May the Lord give you strength to live the Gospel daily and to bear witness of the Gospel to others.

May the Lord bless the sick.

O God Almighty, You are the owner of every creature and of every unclean spirit, free all people from demoniacal influence, from the influence of sin and evil.

O Lord, illumine our minds, give us your light, save us all, our families, our parishes, bless Italy, bless the Church, especially those responsible for the Church, the Pope, the Bishops, the Priests, the religious, bless the whole world.

Lord Jesus Christ, we pray for this woman, make her free and give her your light, your peace, the freedom of heart.

Come Lord Jesus Christ! come into her soul and stay with her for ever, be her protection, be her life. Ensure, Lord Jesus Christ, that

this person may be a witness of your redemption, free her from every evil. Lord Jesus Christ, we pray for this person to be freed from any demoniacal influence, from any sin, any psychical illness, from anything troubling her life.
Be for her redemption and protection.
Thank you Jesus.

(Fr. Tomislav Vlašić - 9 September 1985)

Accept Our Lady's announcement and everything else will be changed

... On 15 August Our Lady said She was entrusted to give the world a solemn blessing. What does a solemn blessing mean? It means everything. When God gives us His blessing, everything changes. And, as Our Lady was giving Her blessing on 4 August, satan could not possibly be present there, in Medjugorje. When Our Lady gives Her special blessing, something fundamental in us is changed.

I have personally experienced this blessing, for grace becomes tangible.

Many a time, as I went to Medjugorje, consumed by my work, I used to come away changed. Our Lady was giving us Her special blessing and a fundamental change was felt in the group. And so, when Our Lady says, « Pray, pray, pray », it means, in my eyes, invoking this divine blessing. I have come to realise that we make far too many human efforts and too few supernatural ones – that is asking, praying, begging God to give us grace. When God gives us His blessing, everything changes.

To explain this better – people usually, when coming to Medjugorje, ask specific questions and expect from Our Lady some sort of reply in the form of a recipe. This is not what Our Lady gives, but rather, She directs us towards God, towards the Holy Spirit. We must be open to God, then God will change the state of the world, of our souls.

Did you hear last Thursday's message?

Our Lady said that satan's plan had failed and begged us to carry on praying for Her divine plan to be fully fulfilled.

During the period of the last four years, I can truly say that Our Lady has been teaching us to pray. Christian life consists – from what I have understood – of a continuous deepening of prayer, since prayer is meeting God, uniting with God, becoming bound together with God in a life bond.

Our Lady leads us forward in the deepening of this need for prayer. When people are told that Our Lady wishes for prayer, they understand phrases like – seven Our Father's, the Rosary…., but this is not the message of Our Lady. Admittedly, Our Lady has invited us to pray seven Our Father's, Hail Mary's and Glory Be's, to pray the Rosary, to live the Eucharist. However, Our Lady has also taught us how to enter into the full depth of prayer.

In our prayer group we practised the Our Father alone for more than half of Lent; we received the task of practising just the Our Father so that we could enter into every word of the Our Father, so that the Our Father – as Our Lady says – may become a continuous melody inside our hearts. Our Lady taught us to meditate on the Gospel, to meditate on the mysteries of the Rosary, She taught us how to prepare ourselves for the Eucharist, how to live it. Therefore, you can understand how Our Lady has not only given us the forms of prayer, but She has also wished us to enter into the full depth of prayer, and the depth of prayer consists of the actual total encounter with God, of what happens when two people unite. Our Lady gave the prayer group a short prayer, a prayer which should be lived continuously, « *My soul is full of love like the sea, my heart is full of peace like the river; I am not a saint, but I am invited to be one* ».

Our Lady talks a lot on this very point – I am not a saint, I must be humble, I must recognise my sins. However, it is very important not to be crushed by one's sins, not to lay too much weight on them, not to dwell on the analysis of such sins, but to make a fresh start forward as soon as possible. In every sin you must discover the fact that you are invited to become saints and to run forward.

This message has been repeated by Our Lady many a time and we have come to realise that it is satan who is crushing us with our sins – he judges, he condemns, he always condemns the person or the people who brood on their sins, who leave room for the devil. The devil acts through too much analysing, too many judgements.

Our Lady says, «*It is sufficient for you to look at your sin in earnest and then quickly to move forward to correct such a sin*». This is paramount. We have discovered lately how so many people get crushed by a sense of guilt, and they do not move forward, they do not change. Our Lady wants to urge us towards hope, so that we may move forward from each sin, so that the sin committed may act as a step towards God.

In a message given to Jelena Our Lady said a phrase, which I have called an interesting play on words, «*Your humility must be proud. Your pride must be humble*». I am telling you of this message to complete the picture of what I was saying a moment ago, so as not be crushed by sin on both sides, since we must be proud of God's gifts.

Many people do not practise humility in the right spirit. People are not sincerely humble. They say, «But I am not capable, I am not like that...».

Our Lady says, «*If you have received a gift from God you must be proud of it. However, do not say it is yours, but say it is God's*». I have discovered in this the foundation stone for the spiritual dynamics because I see Our Lady wanting our inner self to flourish. One must never be in a negative, but always in a positive state. We must be well pleased when we possess some gifts. She has given us the task of discovering in ourselves the gifts we have received from God and of living them. In my opinion this is vital for a positive dynamic in our spiritual life.

And now I want to tell you something else about the pilgrims.

Many pilgrims who have heard the news of Medjugorje, of the miracles, come here to look for something for themselves. In my view, this is all very dangerous, as in this way the centre of one's spiritual life becomes displaced.

During confessions I have experienced that so many people appear to be deaf, unable to receive advice, for they were only thinking of themselves, searching for something, for healing, consolation etc. They were incapable of changing their lives and this is a great mistake, contrary to what Jesus said, «Look first of all for the Kingdom of God and everything else will be granted unto you».

That is why I insist so much on people welcoming in earnest Our Lady's messages and Her presence. This should be something essential. Our Lady has appeared in this very important period of our history, She has appeared to tell us important and urgent things – peace, prayer, fasting, sacramental life, urgent conversion.

Our Lady has appeared. She has become tangible for the visionaries; it is a serious matter, that a being of the hereafter should present Herself on this earth, and if we in earnest, in faith, welcome the event, then diseases, death and troubles carry no more weight. I therefore want to tell you to accept Our Lady's appeal and everything else will then be changed.

Another message I would like to give you pilgrims is this – do not be muddlers. Satan is a muddler, a deceiving being. Many people live in confusion. When will the Church give her final definition? What has this Bishop said? What are that journalist and this theologian saying?

People live in confusion. All I want to say is this – do not live in confusion. Confusion comes from satan.

God gives light to each one of us, so that we may discern. If you have doubts, then put these doubts in the hands of God through prayer. Our Lady Herself when meeting the Angel had a few doubts, but She addressed them to Him who can solve them, to God, and from God the answer came: « Be not afraid ».

I invite the pilgrims, therefore, not to discuss the events, not to argue about the apparitions of Our Lady, but to place one's problems, one's doubts in God's hands and to pray, and God will give each one of us the light.

In order to solve this problem of doubt, I want to give you some other reasons which will help you to feel secure. I will say only a few words – follow the facts, the ectasies of the visionaries of Medjugorje. They are described in a most serious, scientific way. Never have the ecstasies of the Church ever been described in such a scientific way as these have. You can watch the relevant films, read the book by the French medical team and you will see that the ecstasies are a fact. At that particular moment the visionaries live outside time and space. When we are faced with a very important matter, then we have to adopt a serious attitude towards it. Scripture teaches us that the fear of God is the beginning of wisdom. In front of such a mystery we must be kneeling, must be serious and ask God for an explanation. We cannot enter the mystery, the content of what the visionaries feel, but must accept the explanation on moral and scientific grounds.

It is the only way along which all saints have walked. If we put into controversy all the stones of this path, of this road, then we will also have put the Christian name into discussion.

And finally, I would like to tell you that I have been observing all the criticism and attacks on Medjugorje. In my opinion, if anybody had been analysed and criticised as much as Medjugorje has, they would by now have been declared insane. If one had been looking for negative sides in any person in that same manner, one would have found so many, as to be able to destroy such a person. According to my experience, the deepest, most positive aspect of it all, is that, during the last four years, I have come across problems which could not possibly be solved by human logic, by human strength and yet, each time God has intervened in a most marvellous way; of this, I am a witness.

We cannot forget Good Friday 1983 when I wanted to write a letter of protest about certain things; I wrote it and laid it on the table. I was waiting for a lawyer to correct it. Nobody knew of it except the Parish Priest.

On the Monday, Jelena, without knowing, came up to me and said, « Do not turn to anybody for help. When you have problems you must keep smiling and in prayer. When God starts a work nobody can stop Him ».

This is vital and that is why Our Lady is always telling us, « *Pray, fast, leave it in the hands of God* ».

It is much easier for me to fast every day on bread and water than to leave it in the hands of God. Leaving it in the hands of God ought to be a fruit of fasting and prayer. And he who has really experienced this, that is, leaving everything to God, enjoys immense happiness and endless peace.

(Fr. Tomislav Vlašić - 10 September 1985)

To consecrate oneself to the Cross

I can tell you of many experiences.

First of all, as far as the messages of Our Lady are concerned, it is quite clear that the events of Medjugorje are facts. Our Lady has appeared, the Woman clad in the sun, fighting against satan.

From the beginning of July to the end of August almost all messages have been a warning of satan's presence and we, here in Medjugorje, have experienced just this. It is not a question of items of news from a newspaper, but a question of real happenings, after which we were able to experience satan's attacks, his real presence. For Her part, Our Lady teaches us to face this problem, how to fight it and She always points out to us the weapons – prayer, penance, inner spiritual life – by which we are able to face the problem of satan's presence. We have, in fact, lived through one of satan's revelations, not so much in the sense of a new revelation, but in the sense that, through these messages, Our Lady has made us rediscover satan's presence.

And we have opened our eyes and seen him and learned something very, very important, in my opinion, for the whole Church, since through these warnings of Our Lady we have discovered satan's presence, really hidden in civilization which has denied satan's presence, just as it has denied God's presence.

The other experiences are more those of spiritual dynamics. Whenever I can, I work in Medjugorje mainly with those groups formed by Our Lady – the prayer groups. I cannot talk now about the messages given to the prayer groups, but what I can say is that a profound plan on the part of Our Lady and of God is involved whereby people grow in a very healthy way and the fruits of this spiritual path are there already to be seen: at the same time a vital revelation has become clear to us. For instance, during all this period of time we have been experiencing what happens to people who have practised yoga when they enter the Medjugorje area. They all suffer from some sort of breakdown, that is, they all feel some considerable distress. By following, for instance, those who have been practising yoga, I have personally discovered many limitations.

We have discovered what Jesus Christ means in the face of yoga. We have also discovered why these people, as they enter the area where a strong grace is present, experience inner distress.

First of all we have discovered that yoga is a human technique: it is a human kind of wisdom and it brings people up to a certain limit, where people stop and stay, without going any further.

Another problem we have discovered is this – people following the yoga techniques open themselves and become totally open, the total opening being such as to allow beings to enter. There is even a possibility that evil beings may enter, but it is usually the case of the guru, the master, the one who directs the person.

The limitation of yoga is the human limit, whereby, with the aid of a technique my body can be made ready to reach silence, but it will not go any further.

As St. John has pointed to Jesus Christ, similarly, yoga's point of arrival can only be that human limit, after which the open person ought to make room for Jesus Christ and for Jesus Christ alone. These ailments come because these people have not actually met the living God who leads to total enlightenment and salvation.

What we have recently experienced is mainly this – on the one hand we have discovered that those who live a spiritual technique strive to get to some sort of concentration, silence, to attain a calm attitude. On the other hand, in these days, it has also become clear to us that we are given certain disturbances, temptations, because – as we have found out through the visionaries – God allows these very disturbances, these very temptations, in order to bring us to total purification.

So there you have a spiritual path, the one of yoga, following human foot-prints and reaching the human limit, whereas we, in our opening up to faith, go beyond human limits.

It is God who allows even misfortunes, who allows even trials, through which we are able to go beyond.

This I have learned: yoga gives us silence. Christ gives us peace. Peace which goes beyond silence. This confirms what Our Lady told us through Jelena in 1983 – that She indeed has come to purify all the world movements and to lead us to Jesus Christ. This is one of our experiences. As far as Medjugorje is concerned, I see this as being of paramount importance, namely, that those priests who have lived this experience of Medjugorje themselves may help those who have been in the East looking for salvation, and bring them to Jesus Christ, without denying certain values of yoga, of oriental human wisdom, but setting out as priests with these people, just like Jesus Christ used to do with the Apostles, in order to bring them to total enlightenment.

How sad I am! Indeed I am sad, because we are too few here in Medjugorje to help people coming from every part of the world in search of God. Many are those who write to me on the very issue of the spiritual level of yoga asking for help, asking to be guided, and I cannot do anything since I am so committed in the parish...

In this spiritual field alone, experts are needed who live interiorly these messages of Our Lady in order to enlighten those who, somehow, have got lost, who have lost their way, who have not fully found God. This is connected with something else; some people have been to India searching for yoga, whilst the whole of the West lives yoga – the Orientals live according to techniques, whereas the Western Christians live the yoga of pleasure: they smoke, drink, eat, enjoy themselves, they want a pleasant Christianity. People in the East look directly for a spiritual path, whereas in the West, those who believe in Christ say they believe in Jesus Christ, but at the same time, look for Christ in pleasure. I have discovered the medieval asceticism – indeed these days I have understood that I can deepen my relationship with God in prayer, only to the degree in which I mortify myself, just as Jesus explained to us yesterday, in the Gospel. He openly started telling the Apostles what one has to bear in mind, « He who is prepared to lose his life will gain it ».

The meaning of penance, the meaning of fasting is just this. Particularly during the last few months, Our Lady and also Jesus have been asking through Jelena – particularly some group members – to consecrate themselves to the Cross. Our Lady's last message is also indeed a call to the consecration to the Cross, the kind of consecration whereby Jesus wishes there were people willing to consecrate everything, ready to really offer everything to God.

In my opinion we shall reach once more a spiritual depth along this path. Why have many monasteries remained empty? As I see it, they have, because they have lost mystical prayer and in turn, mystical prayer has been lost because we have lost the meaning of fasting and deep prayer.

Now, with these experiences we are making our way towards a spiritual, mystical life from which many a vocation will stem.

... I know we are strong when we are close to God and that we can solve problems to the degree in which we are close to God, but as so many Christians are far from prayer, they are also far from God.

We have learned to live, to have our own lives in God, to feel that when we are closer to God, we are really closer to life, we are more complete.

But since we are not quite so close to God through prayer, we are not even able to choose God's means, to choose God's weapons against evil.

Let us start praying, let us learn prayer and we shall, day by day, discover within ourselves a greater strength, a brighter light.

Every day we shall have more life.

If we manage to discover exactly what Our Lady teaches us and if that becomes tangible for us, a true life experience, then we will also be able to bring salvation to the whole world.

It is useless to bring Our Lady's messages to the world as we would bring the messages of newspapers or books, because Bibles and the most beautiful written works are to be found everywhere, but these are lifeless without us. Without a deep and serious commitment through conversion, Our Lady's word has no meaning.

I would like to invite everyone to live this deep reality, through daily prayer, through conversion.

(Fr. Tomislav Vlašić - 16 September 1985)

Ask God questions

People are used to asking the Fathers, the visionaries questions – yes, this too is necessary, but you must ask your questions where you will get complete answers – search for God, ask God your questions, in order to get to know God, in order to reach God. Now, when I tell you to « ask a question », I mean, above all, « Ask God your questions » in order to obtain the answer.

I shall try and explain. There are people who do not pray to God, who do not address themselves to God, since they are not sure whether He exists. Yesterday I had a meeting of about an hour with someone who has finished his theological studies, has got involved in Christian life and then forsaken everything, including faith. He is in darkness, does not know God, does not feel the need to pray to God. To-day, I say to those who feel like that person before God, incapable of praying, of knowing if God exists or not, « Ask God your questions, look for God ». None of us, even though an unbeliever, can disengage himself from asking God these questions. On the day of the Assumption, Mirjana had a talk with Our Lady, in which Our Lady was expressing Her grief and saying how awful the unbelievers will feel when they come face to face with God.

A year ago I asked the same visionary, « Why does Our Lady feel so sorry for unbelievers? Those who have not known God are not even responsible ». The visionary replied, « Our Lady says: *"Every adult has the ability to know God, the sin of the world consists of this – in not searching for God"* ».

The sin of the world is that it does not care for God, it does not search for God. This is why I say to those among you who do not feel like praying: « search for God ». You can get to know Him if you commit yourselves as much as one commits oneself to physical matters, by penetrating their physical laws. If you place yourselves at God's disposal in order to get to know one thing, one Being Who is there for our salvation, for your eternal life, then you will know Him, as each one of us has received the ability from God to know Him, because we are made according to His image.

That is why I said at the beginning – look for God and ask God questions.

I then say to all of you – ask God your questions. People coming to Medjugorje are busy meeting the visionaries, asking questions in order to get answers. From the answers you might receive from the visionaries, you will not find the right answers for yourself. You may obtain some indication, some arrow, some word to drive you forward. I have been following what the visionaries have been saying when they were reporting Our Lady's reply to their questions. Our Lady did not give anybody a definite answer, such as, « I will heal you, I will save you », or « I will solve your problem »; never did She give a definite answer, but said, « *Have faith in God, pray and fast, have faith* ».

Our Lady directs us towards God and it is up to us to ask God questions through fasting and prayer, through the search for God, in order to be enlightened in our hearts, in order to receive the true answer. Without this obedience to Our Lady to carry on this programme of confidence, of abandonment to God, we will not obtain an answer. That is why I say to you, « Ask God your questions ».

It now seems to me that when I say, « Ask God your questions », we go beyond the prayer we usually say. We often say prayers without asking, without asking for discernment; we say a prayer without knowing what we have been saying and what to answer to God.

We really must ask questions and receive answers in prayer.

In a message Our Lady told little Jelena, for the benefit of the prayer group, that after every prayer we must hear God's answer. That is why I ask you to ask questions, but they have to be the right questions and be made before He who can give you a true answer.

When I tell you to ask questions, I am telling you to pray in the proper manner. In my opinion, judging at least by what I have been experiencing in prayer lately, the most important thing is actually wanting to accept what God gives us.

For me, this theme is very important and very deep.

I shall explain – many people pray, but do not want to accept what God is offering us. Here is a practical example: we pray « Thy kingdom come » and we do not want His kingdom; we pray, « Thy will be done » and we go against His will; we look for forgiveness, « as we forgive those who trespass against us », but we do not want to forgive.

We do not want to take the gifts, and if we do not want to take what God offers us, then our prayer is closed. There can be no results if there is no opening up to what the Lord is truly offering us. Consequently we cannot receive « the rest » either.

Jesus told us various parables and promised to give us all that is necessary for our salvation. He also gave us the following rule: « Look first of all for the Kingdom of God, and everything else will be granted unto you ». If I do not want His Kingdom, then neither can I gather His fruits.

In my opinion, the most important thing in prayer is seeing that God is at our disposal, is wanting to take the gifts that the Lord gives us. And I feel – I mean myself – like the eldest son of the Father; the prodigal son has gone, but the eldest son is at home and unable to help himself to the good things the Father gives him. I really feel that way, as a priest, as a religious.

God has given me everything, all the graces are at my disposal and I am not capable of taking or of enjoying them.

It is a tragedy of our Christian life, of our not taking these things. A nun came to complain, saying, « Father, I feel crushed, I feel a dryness within me, I am too busy in the hospital. I pray very little, I cannot find the time – what can you say to me? ».

I told her, « I am sorry. Jesus chose you to give you His love and you do not take it. You have been particularly chosen by Jesus Christ and you have been left without that love; why are you living so poorly, when God has chosen you in such a special way? ».

I am not saying this only for the nun, but for myself as well; I am always poor when I am unable to make use of this love of His, to experience this love, and all of us Christians are poor, miserable, when we are unable to take, to accept this love and to live it.

And how can you take it? Just think for a moment of all you say in your prayers, in your Our Father's and desire with all your heart for what you say — that they may not be just empty pharisaic words! When you say, Hail Mary, think for a moment with deepest admiration, Holy Mary full of grace, blessed are You, pray for us sinners. A deep desire to reach out for God, to be with God, as the Virgin has been with God.

If you want to reach the point where you discover that all things, all graces are at your disposal, just move with simplicity, with humility towards the word of the Gospel: read a little of the Gospel every day and put the words of the Gospel into practice.

There God puts Himself at your disposal. If we put the words of the Gospel into practice in our lives, then the path opens itself to us. You heard advice yesterday, in the Gospel according to Luke, to pay attention, « He who has will be given even more ».

He who practises faith, he who opens himself through every day's practice, to him will the path be opened. And he will realise — yes, my Father's gifts are at my disposal and I am capable of taking them. This is the wisdom of Our Lady leading us to simplicity, humility, and with such simplicity, to pick up every word of the Gospel, every word of God.

I repeat — ask God your questions. I would like to underline, at this stage, the difference between a believer and an unbeliever. Even when we are dealing with Christians there are unbelievers as well as believers; even when dealing with people who have come on a pilgrimage, even with people taking part at Mass, there are believers and unbelievers.

I am thinking of those who are open to the Word of God and those who are not. I am making this difference, since the unbelievers tend to discuss, to argue the messages, to attack others, to fight against others in order to bring their own conviction to others. This is being unfaithful. Our Lady became faithful by asking God questions. Initially She was unable to grasp God's plan, « How can this be since I have no husband? ». She asked questions, She did not set about discussing with others, attacking others, discussing with the high priest or with the pharisees. But, in the presence of God, she started asking questions, and the light came to Her from God. When Our Lady teaches us, during this period, to pray, pray, pray, it is this She means – to enter into intimacy with God, to ask God deeper and deeper questions and to look for the answers from God in order to be enlightened. I am telling you, from the point of view of the priest who is following the events of Medjugorje and this also applies to the pilgrims – if you want to be real pilgrims, leave your discussions, your arguments, your attacks, the bitterness of your heart behind, just because the others do not accept the apparitions, but ask instead your questions and, if there are doubts in your hearts, place these doubts in such a way as to consult God. If you really have appeared O Virgin, what do you want?

Ask these questions in prayer and you will receive the answers.

In my opinion this is very important and I would say it is everything. If we place ourselves in search of God on a spiritual level and we deepen this daily path, then we are on the way to a true pilgrimage, since the true pilgrimage is the one which continuously leads us towards God.

I wish you to be eternal pilgrims, not for you to go to Medjugorje and go home to be the same as before. If you have, you have made a great mistake, you have tired yourselves out and achieved nothing. I want you to go back home and carry on asking God questions, carry on praying, deepening this intimacy with God. Then you will realise that the apparitions are true and nobody will have to explain it to you. You well know of that meeting between Jesus and the Samaritan woman, when she led other men to the well of Jacob; at first people believed the woman, but then they said, « We believe because we ourselves have discovered, not because you have told us ». And we are all connected with the work of discovering God.

Our Lady has Her own messages and when we discover in our daily lives the presence of God Our Lady brought us, then we will be without doubts and shall be able to announce to others the truth lived by us and shall be witnesses of the apparitions.

However, without this plan of asking and placing ourselves before God as beings in need of the light from God, we shall not reach the end. On a spiritual level nobody can give us inner certainty from without; if this were possible, then all those who saw Jesus' miracles would have been certain, whereas, instead, they wanted to stone Lazarus and Jesus to death.

They saw Lazarus resuscitated, but they did not believe.

Inner certainty, therefore, comes through inner exercise, through inner opening, through the opening of the heart.

Try and open yourselves indeed by wishing to reach God and what God gives us, and the Lord will enlighten you.

Another theme which is related to this is a reply to those who come here asking – how can we organise a prayer group? You can organise a prayer group only on the level of what I have told you. If you wish to pray, if you want to learn what the Lord tells you, if you want to do more for God, if you commit yourselves more to prayer, the way to organise prayer is not important; there are different ways in the Church and you will find out by yourselves the ways within a parish, a community, a convent, a hospital; you will find a thousand ways how to organise, but the most important thing is to be willing to pray, to search for God, to abandon oneself to God and God will intervene in the groups. I am confident about that, since I have experience of several groups.

This way, the Lord also grants special graces, so that the group in question may accomplish a particular mission, but only if our hearts have such fervour as to really put themselves at God's service, seeking to be enlightened, seeking to live every word of the Gospel.

And do not take short cuts in the Gospel, since many lines in the Gospel get omitted, discarded, interpreted in one's own fashion by those who want a Gospel according to their own will; put yourselves totally at the Gospel's disposal and the Lord will guide you.

In the message where Our Lady was warning us of satan's presence it is remarkable that, in every message, She was giving us the weapons to defeat him. The weapons are – prayer and fasting, not discussions or arguments. Therefore, you also must walk, follow this path so that the presence of God which manifests itself in Medjugorje through the Virgin may be clear to you.

I repeat – it will never be clear on a scientific level, since the supernatural cannot be argued with science, nor can it be demonstrated.

But I am telling you this much – the apparitions of Medjugorje are being investigated and carefully elaborated in a scientific way and they are not to be argued about. It is a matter of ecstasy which goes beyond human capabilities.

This is the scientific conclusion of all those who have worked here, including Italian and French doctors who have been researching in the last few weeks. They have unanimously stated that it is an occurence which goes beyond human experience, beyond the capabilities of scientific explanation.

In my opinion it is not enough to say, « It is sufficient for me to believe in the Virgin, I am not interested in the apparitions ». As far as I am concerned this is not enough, because when God appears, when Our Lady appears, a particular gift to mankind is involved.

It is a particular gift – not to accept a gift your mother, sister, financé offers you, to reject such a gift, is hurtful to both.

If Our Lady comes at a critical moment for mankind and tells us urgent and important things for the whole of mankind, but men still remain the same; I then feel this as a great sin – it is rejecting the grace of God.

It is not a great sin in a preceptive sense, but it is so as a resistance to the Holy Spirit. The pharisees knew all the laws well and practised them, but they went against the Spirit and that is why they crucified Jesus Christ.

Let us be careful not to be closed, blocked from the Holy Spirit.

The Heavenly Mother is not bringing other presents – She has presented Herself as the Mother who awakes us – get up, it is time to work, it is time to be on guard.

Get up, pray, be converted.

She does not add anything new, but She urges us along the grace She received from God and wants to help us, wants to save us.

Pray, ask God your questions, the questions of salvation, so that the Holy Spirit may enlighten all of you, may descend upon everyone as He came down upon the Virgin Mary.

(Fr. Tomislav Vlašić - 24 September 1985)

God has decided to purify the world

If you look at the Gospels of the last few Sundays, what has Jesus been talking about? Jesus has been talking of His and our own suffering.

Jesus started telling the Apostles openly that He was to suffer, not with the intention of putting them into a crisis or of frightening them, but so that they might know that they would have to go through the Cross, through suffering. When we hear this word we are made aware of the fact that we have to go through the Cross, through suffering.

If we are not aware of this reality, then we are not true Christians. This is where the pilgrim's problem appears, a problem which, if unsolved, is a source of fear, but if solved, becomes hope for the future.

Yesterday I read in a Croation monthly published in West Germany that last year four hundred million marks have been allocated to abortion. Who will pay for this before God? Who will? We will. All of us.

I just gave you one example. Who will pay for the drug addicts? Who will pay for those killed? Who will pay for those dying of starvation? All this is injustice on earth which must be paid for. We live in a civilization which is virtually without God. Unfortunately, we Christians too, we live on the whole a life of atheism. And if we Christians do nothing to bring people towards hope, then we are left with a terribly hard Cross.

Therefore, to look ahead at a future which will be beautiful means to look at a world without sin. If we, at this moment, when Our Lady is inviting us, do not see these sins and the need for conversion, penance, prayer, then we have not understood the times we live in.

There is no need for us to fear the future, but we do need to look at the future in the light of faith, of supernatural life and we do need to commit ourselves to the world's future, so that men may be saved and life on earth may be more beautiful.

But this will be difficult if the world is to carry on living without God.

I am sure that, from all these messages, God has decided to purify the world. If we are converted then this purification will be easy; but if the world will not be converted, if it is not prepared to accept the programme of God, then God will go ahead by means of sacrifices and these sacrifices will not be voluntary. You must be realistic – if you want to renovate your house, see how many difficulties there are, and when God wants to put this world right, which is living in atheism, how many difficulties are we then faced with! We must be realistic and look at the future with realism but with peace; if you want to find once again your peace in looking at the future, then you must become « voluntary sacrifices ». Many, out of their own will, chose sacrifices, fasting, sufferings for God, so that God may save the world.

This is the reality of the Gospel, when Jesus plainly told the Apostles that He has to suffer. He willingly took the sacrifice upon himself in order to save His brothers, because through sacrifice – the one in which we offer everything to God – we do the best thing before God. For this reason Our Lady invites us to fast, for this very reason Our Lady invites us to conversion, to point out a radical decision to follow God, to belong to God.

Talking of suffering, the Gospel says you have to cut off your hand, you have to cut off your leg; theorists say that this is too much. But this is not too much. If you have a ruined limb, you tell the doctor, « Cut it off to save my life ». « Get rid of my eye in order to save the other one, in order to save my life ». This is the way we have to behave before eternal life. If we do not behave in this way before eternal life, we are not realistic, we do not wish to save our lives; we want to save one hundred thousand liras, we want to save something, we want to save a car, but not our lives. Try and clear out your homes of all the superfluous wealth.

You will realise the need to cut things out all the time – to cut habits out, to cut time out, to cut things out, to cut pleasures out; how many things there are that need to be cut out!

If we are able to remove so many things, so many programmes, so many wishes, then we will come around to understanding the joy of suffering on which we must meditate on Friday, the Feast of St. Francis.

You will be in a position to welcome the Word of God only to the degree in which you will have been able to renounce things, in which you will have done penance; therefore penance combined with prayer is worth more. They are two paths – without prayer, fasting is lame, without fasting, prayer is lame, whereas both help us and drive us forward. For this reason Our Lady has particularly recommended that we should fast. There are people who are unable to fast on bread and water; however nobody is exempt from fasting. There are a thousand ways to fast.

One must fast, because our body which is constantly worried about nourishment, money, pleasures, needs to be emptied like one does when one is under treatment; it needs to be purified also with regard to spiritual life, so that we do not worry if we spend a whole day without eating, but are rather like Jesus in the desert who, after forty days was not worried, but could bear up to it because He was living on the Word of God.

This is the sense of penance, of fasting, the sense of sacrifice, and another thing – if you want to go forward and follow Our Lady – then make some voluntary sacrifices.

Those four hundred million marks need to be compensated, must be paid for, let us make sacrifices for the sins of the world.

Without this, we will not have understood Mass, as Mass is not only the sacrifice of Jesus Christ, but it must also be my sacrifice united with the one of Jesus Christ, my blood, my sweat united with the one of Jesus Christ. Then Mass becomes what Jesus meant it should be.

(Fr. Tomislav Vlašić - 29 September 1985)

« I am giving you my love so that you may give it to others »

I greet you all, welcome.

I will bring you up to date with the situation here.

Many ask what the Commission has done; the Commission had a meeting at the end of September, on 26 and 27. Two more doctors, neuropsychiatrists, have now joined and have compiled a statement which has not yet been published. They merely said, « There will be a further meeting at the end of November ». The members of the Commission have reported what has come out of the last of their meetings.

Bishop Žanić greeted them at the beginning of the meeting and left them to their work.

Father Ivan Dugandžić, newly arrived here, has been a member of the Commission since the start.

He is a Franciscan and has been Master of novices for six years in Humac; he has studied the Bible a lot.

He has come to replace me as I am appointed to another parish now, but I still come up nearly every day to give a hand for the Italian and French pilgrims.

Fr. Ivan Dugandžić knows the situation very well and he has been saying that one can now feel another atmosphere, a positive one, within the commission.

A month ago, doctors from Milan and Turin came here, about fifteen in all and made quite a few experiments.

This is very important for us, despite it being sometimes a bit of a nuisance for the visionaries, who are not at all happy about doctors coming round for experiments.

The latest result will be published as soon as possible. One thing can be said – all doctors have once again confirmed that we are faced with an inexplicable phenomenon.

That is to say, that medicine, psychology, parapsychology, neuro-psychiatry, every science, has reached its own limit and cannot go any further. In what sense? They have established that the visionaries are healthy both in mind and body.

I have told you that there are small problems with Vicka and Marija sometimes, but this is not relevant, as they are not ill in the sense of a definite illness. Doctors have stated, « During the apparition the visionaries find themselves in a contradictory, inexplicable situation ». The doctors made experiments with pain – before the apparitions a normal reaction similar to pain was registered, whilst during the ecstasy the pain diminished by four hundred per cent, almost narcosis, anaesthesia, and here on the other hand, we have a normal activity of the brain. It is not a state of dreaming or anything else. I asked the doctors whether there is anything else we can do in this respect. They replied, « Hardly anything, it seems to us there is no need ».

Then we can effectively say that we have performed all possible experiments and they have all confirmed that we are faced with something inexplicable. Beyond this limit comes faith, one can either accept their testimony of the last fifty-one months or throw everything away.

In the last few days an Italian parapsychologist has been here once again. He has already written articles in a few newpapers. He once spoke to a nun in church.

When he went home to listen to his tape, a voice got between his questions and the nun's answer, saying, « I have come to Medjugorje ». When he heard this, he was puzzled – he knew nothing of Medjugorje. He listened a few times over again and started to become interested. He arrived here on 4 April 1984 and got the visionaries to listen to the tape; they could not say they recognised the voice, but asked Our Lady and received a positive answer. He told me many a time he was a rationalist atheist and wanted to forget this inexplicable story, as it is common in parapsychology. This year he has been having three or four new experiences – the same thing. He once went to church on his own taking a small tape recorder with him, speaking very close to it and, once again he received interferences related to Medjugorje.

On Saturday morning he came to me and said, « I could not sleep all night; I have meditated a lot on the explanation and, he said, this is the most logical one for me and I am positive it cannot be undue influence ».

For he who is asking whether it is a voice from Heaven, an influenced answer might be, « Yes, it is a voice from Heaven », but the answer was, « It is a gift for him ».

« This is the most logical one – he said – since Our Lady is the Mother, She does not criticise ». He added, « I could have expected, "You must believe, you must pray, you must confess" », in other words, a lesson. Nothing of the sort. Only, « This is a gift for him ». He left saying, « I now feel more open-minded, but I must still meditate a lot on this ».

There will be a congress of parapsychologists in Italy and he will report on all these things.

I am telling you this so that you may see how very interesting this is for us, how all this is lasting and how more and more pilgrims come, not only from Italy, but from all over the world.

There is a saying here with us – for every miracle three days are enough. But it seems to me that, for this miracle they are not enough, and more and more come from all over the world. How can one explain this? Only that Our Lady is speaking as a Mother, and people come. All I know is that when you come here, we have nothing for you and yet one can see people finding something essential. It does not matter how other things seem, afterwards. And so, now and again things happen to bring a new stimulus. For this very parapsychologist a very great stimulus has taken place and he, in his own terms, will tell the world.

Now we must ask ourselves – why does all this happen? Our Lady in a message to Jelena, said, « *When the Lord comes He does not come for fun, He comes in earnest* ». All these graces, healings, conversions, all this happens to make us think a little.

The main message is Peace.

Our Lady has come and invited us all to peace and told us Her name, « *I am the Queen of Peace* ».

And here I always say unceasingly – we can rest assured, looking at all these experiences, all the messages that the Lord, through Our Lady, has made us responsible for peace and we must allow ourselves to be made responsible.

Peace. We are not just talking here of the absence of wars; this also, but peace in a broader sense; peace in the Bible means all aspects of well being, physical, psychical and spiritual, the whole lot. So therefore, if we want peace now we cannot say, « There is nothing we can do if there is a war in Asia ». It is not just absence of wars, it is peace of the heart, it is reconciliation between myself and God and then between myself and others.

If we do not accept the peace of the Lord, we cannot bring it to the world and each one of us is responsible in this respect.

If we start by being reconciled in our families, at work, then we can increasingly bring the world, even by centimetre or millimetre forward, closer to peace.

And if we all start, peace will come.

And if we do not start, we Christians cannot find excuses for not starting.

A few months ago Marija Pavlović retired for a week to pray and rest. She told us that the apparitions had been a little longer and that during one apparition she asked Our Lady, « Have you something concrete for me? ». Our Lady replied, « *Yes I have. I give you my love so that you may give it to others* ». And this is the logic of Our Lady and of the Lord with regard to us.

What more do we want if Our Lady tells not only Marija but all of us, « *I give you my love, so that you may give it to others?* ».

But in order to give love to others one must accept it in the first place; I am sure that each one of us, every man wants to accept love.

And now another question – how, how must I live? What is Our Lady asking of me so that I may live this – I may accept love and bring it to others?

Our Lady is asking for prayer, fasting and conversion. I have been talking to many pilgrims and it appears we have all become experts in finding excuses not to pray.

It seems to me that Our Lady will not accept these excuses. She is calling us and many wonder where they can find the time. A lady asked me this morning, « Why is it that we have to pray this way? ». I noticed she was sincerely looking for an answer. I know that many cannot pray for three hours, as they have to work, but I also know something else – we can all start the way Our Lady started off here. Quite simply – the Creed, seven Our Father's, Hail Mary's, Glory Be's and one day of fasting; She then asked for other things. I know of a few people who have told me that they seem to find time more easily for the whole Rosary now than they did for the Creed and the seven Our Father's at the beginning.

What has happened? It is not a matter of the day having twenty five hours for these families, just because we now have one more hour for prayer. No, that is not the case, as when one starts praying one realises one does have the time.

What is prayer? Prayer is life with God, the Rosary is above all life with Our Lady, Our Mother.

By repeating and by meditating the mysteries we are drawn nearer to Her life, to Jesus' life. And if someone wonders: « Why should one be with Mother? » he will not have the time to stay every day with Mother half an hour in the morning or one hour in the evening.

And now a few facts about the latest messages.

In the last message Our Lady has asked as to learn afresh how to be thankful and this request of Hers is deeply connected with all the messages. If we start thanking one another, even for the smallest things, we shall have peace in our families.

Look, how does as wife feel if a husband who has come home from work starts shouting, « What have you been doing? You are doing nothing; these chores of yours are worth nothing ». How does she feel? Awful. There comes the conflict. However, if the husband sees that she has cleaned even the smallest of things and says,

« Thank you », the wife will have the joy and strength to do even greater things. But we are experts in seeing what does not get done and then the conflicts come.

How many conflicts would have been saved in families if only youngsters could have seen what parents have done for them. If they do not see, they want more and more.

Thus comes peace and in this way one can spread it. One must also pray in order to be granted the gift to be thankful, to be able to say, « Thank you »; one needs humility, acknowledgement of the other, ability to see him.

Our Lady is asking for another concrete thing – to live the messages in humility. I shall explain this briefly. It is irrelevant to say, « I was born in Medjugorje » or « I have been to Medjugorje »; one thing alone is relevant – to live the messages. Our Lady has basically asked for a consecration to the Cross. She said, « *Pray before the Cross; there you will receive many graces. Consecrate yourselves to the Cross and promise not to swear at Jesus in the Cross* ».

When our faith becomes personal faith, I am dealing with my Father, my Mother, my Jesus, my Cross, my Church, my Faith – I shall not be able to swear, it will just not be possible.

And if you consecrate yourselves to the Cross, not only can I say, « do not swear and do not offend », but a great deal more than that; when you hear some swear word in the street or on the bus or on a train, you will even be able to bless the Lord, to pray for someone swearing. You can therefore see how Our Lady is asking for all these positive things.

Lastly, I want to tell you this – Our Lady has never said that we should ask for peace, for love from others, but always, as in the reply to Marija, « *I give you, so that you may give. I give you peace, love and you must give it to others* ».

If we Christians start living this way, you will see the whole world opened to this reality. Many ask for peace, love, reconciliation from others, and who can give it? This too is conversion – seeing that the Lord is giving us much so that we in turn give much – when we have grasped this, our life will change as Our Lady also wishes.

(Fr. Slavko Barbarić - 7 October 1985)

It is necessary to be converted immediately

First of all I would like to emphasise this – you have all come to Medjgorje and I believe you all believe in the apparitions.

I must, however, express my sorrow – many a time, in meeting people, mostly individually, I have felt sad. People say, « Yes, we do believe in the apparitions », but I have noticed they do not actually accept the apparitions; they do not accept the messages and I have come across some souls who are very, very hard inside. This is just to express the difficulties of today's world – we are all rather influenced by atheism and even though we are in the Church, our hearts are still hard and unable to welcome what God is telling us through the Church, through the Priests, through Our Lady. When Israel was heading towards the Promised Land, she saw many signs in the sky, on the mountain and many wanted to go back to Egypt...

They stayed and roamed around for forty years and eventually were late in arriving at the Promised Land.

On my part, I wish us all to walk at this moment like God wants us to.

Today's Gospel and the first reading from Jonas explain everything – when a prophecy comes one must not wait for Nineveh's destruction, but one must be converted immediately.

Upon people's conversion will depend whether Nineveh will be destroyed or not. What the world's future will be depends on the world's conversion, that is why biblical prophecies are always conditional – if Nineveh is converted she will not be destroyed.

Therefore, let us not say, « I believe in the apparitions ». It is better to say, « I am doing what Our Lady says ». If I do what Our Lady says, I believe in the apparitions; whereas if I talk about the apparitions and say I believe in them, but do not change, then my word is false, I do not help others, since truth is not inside me.

On this point I want to tell you – try and welcome the apparitions and the messages in earnest. I wish to emphasise two points.

One – If, in the face of these events, you believe in at least ten per cent of the apparitions, when Our Lady says through the visionaries that the world is in a crisis, that world peace is in a crisis, that we have to be converted to obtain peace, that we have to start praying and fasting in order to avoid catastrophes, then we must take Her seriously. But we must also take Her seriously from the point of view of the path in our life, since the only way leading to salvation, fullness of life, is our conversion to God, prayer, fasting and penance.

Another aspect to put us in a serious frame of mind is the following: as we can establish from what the visionaries say, the great events are drawing near. One can see it especially from Marijana's attitude this year – her meetings with Our Lady are more frequent and the visionary explains it by saying, « Because the great events before us are drawing near ».

We must take these events seriously, for we must ponder on what is happening in the world and on what other prophets in the world are saying.

If we look at all this and put it together like a mosaic, then we can clearly see the reality of the future – we must take Our Lady's apparitions seriously.

Another important aspect, as far as I am concerned, as to why one should take Our Lady's apparitions seriously, is the following: the measure of our life is in proportion to our getting closer to God. This is vital. For me, this moment of my life is the last one, it is over, I shall not be able to have it again, and if it is not lived deeply with God, I will have lost a moment of my life. It is a shame to lose one's life. You will remember that a week ago Jesus said in the Gospel that one needs to cut one's arm, one's leg, to remove one's eye to save one's life. And this is not to destroy one's life, but to have it in greater fullness.

The essential nature of Medjugorje in this period, namely, for those who have taken the apparitions seriously, is this – boys, girls, families complain even when praying three or four hours a day. They say, «we pray too little, time flies for us». And that is because they feel in their hearts the flowing of life and, as they get closer to God, they feel more filled with God and with life.

When we experience this – that being close to God means to have life in abundance, then we can race after God and it will not be difficult to remove one's eye, it will not be difficult to cut off a leg, since when I am with God I receive more, I live more fully.

Unfortunately, today's mentality lives in conflict with God. We have placed all our hopes in materialism, in money and that is why we are in a continuous rush, and when we need to pray for five or ten minutes we say, «We have no time». Because we have placed our hope in material things, because of this, tensions stem. When we discover that in God, through prayer, through conversion, we have more life, an abundance of life, then we can go ahead with joy.

I think we cannot find a better example than the one we have been able to see and consider on the feast of St. Francis. He has offered everything and has received everything – a harmony between St. Francis and all creatures, with so many sufferings, yet abundant joy. Death itself is not something ugly – It is the «little sister» embraced by St. Francis.

St. Francis has offered himself totally to God and has received everything from God.

You see, if we take our Christianity seriously, if we take seriously Our Lady who is inviting, urging, admonishing, calling us in order to reach the Gospel, Jesus Christ, we shall truly find life here on earth.

Pilgrims usually ask questions about the future, about what the future will be like, if there will be wars, if there will be troubles. I would like to say to you – do not think of the future in a bad way. Our Lady said in a message, «*The Christian attitude towards the future is the hope of salvation*».

Now, if you wish to have this hope towards the future, you must live this hope, today, totally abandoned to God.

It is not easy, but at the same time, it is.

It is not easy because we have never taken God and the Gospel seriously, we have never taken fasting seriously and prayer seriously in order to be close to God.

It is very easy when we devote time to God, when we are immersed in God's Word, in God's Grace.

Then everything becomes easy – peace and joy are within us and hope comes like a reflection of this reality lived today inside me, just like a reflection, like a fruit of the salvation lived by me today. Today's very moment is vital for living, for our future to be changed. Therefore, « Be converted! ».

From this point of view I must underline the importance for us all to be equally earnest in the face of the apparitions of Medjugorje – those who say, « I believe in Medjugorje's apparitions » and those who say, « I am waiting for what the Church will have to say ». Also those who are not believers – Why? All those who say, « I am a believer », whether they believe in the apparitions or not, they have the duty to turn to God, they have the duty to pray, to live the sacraments; if they do not live this reality, they deceive themselves. Our Lady has only come to awaken us. Our Lady complains about those who say, « I do not believe in God ». « *How difficult it will be for them, when they will approach God's throne and hear His voice saying, "Go to hell"* ».

So there, we are all invited to take the apparitions seriously; let them be at least a starting point for each one of us to look for God, to see if Our Lady is really appearing, if God really exists. If we set out to look for Him, then we shall surely find Him, for we know that God is looking for us, His children, and we well know that the way of getting to know God is the way of practising fasting, daily prayer, community prayer, in order for us to move forward. It is useless to study Christianity with one's intellect if we do not put our faith into practice. Only the opening of our interior selves allows us to attain inner light. You very well know that many have seen the miracles of Jesus Christ but not everyone has had the inner light to know God's presence through the works of Jesus Christ. And this very inner light is what each one of us is lacking.

One comes to this inner light through prayer, through a deep conversion, through a continuous progression of our relationship with God. Then God sends us the Holy Spirit to enlighten us, to recognise God's presence. Without this interior activity we cannot come to the knowledge of Our Lady. You see, when we analyse what the experts have been doing with regard to the ecstasies and apparitions of Medjugorje, in my opinion – and never in history have scientists investigated and studied the apparitions and the ecstasies as in Medjugorje, and like never before have they brought scientific certainty to a supernatural fact – all that is useless if our hearts are not moved, if they do not open themselves.

We must open ourselves and go beyond scientific studies and beyond Our Lady's words, since all Our Lady's messages are signposts on our path – go, pray, read the Gospel, be converted, move on. Our Lady presents Herself like the sign, so that we may be awoken to go, to walk, to discover the light of the Holy Spirit, which is given precisely to the converted heart.

Vicka who is currently listening to an account of the world's future, told me once, « There are some ugly, oppressive things. This is all I can say – that the world must accept Our Lady seriously, must be converted, pray and fast ».

I would like to tell you – carry on your pilgrimage, continue on returning to Italy. Unfortunately, many pilgrims, as they return from a pilgrimage, immediately lose everything, which shows they really have not understood it properly.

On returning to Italy, carry on deepening your pilgrimage towards God and Our Lady and in this way the pilgrimage will have proved itself useful. As you get back to your parishes, gather together, pray, exchange your experiences, carry your testimony essentially with your life, not so much with words, but by carrying peace, hope, joy, the fruits of redemption within yourselves.

I beg you, above all else to pray much because doors open through prayer. Pray for the Sovereign Pontiff, pray for all those responsible for the Church, pray for the whole world, that a continuous blessing may come down from Heaven, and I beg you do not worry when to-morrow you receive certain trials.

When you are surrounded by difficulties, when satan puts you to the test, remember – it is he who is in a crisis, not you.

Since the day Our Lady came, satan is in a crisis, that is why he is angry.

Do carry on with peace, hope, inner certainty; carry on praying. since God, through trials, will bring you to a brighter light and He will indeed, bring the whole world to a brighter light.

(Fr. Tomislav Vlašić - 8 October 1985)

« Confess even the smallest sins, for when you go to meet God, you will suffer for having just one sin inside you »

... There are many pilgrims who come here, not for Our Lady, but for themselves – their ailments, their difficulties, their problems become the centre. Our Lady has come to bring us a plan of salvation from God – we must be resolved to become part of His plan. We know the way only too well. Jesus said, « Look first of all for the Kingdom of God and His justice, the rest will be granted unto you... ». We must, therefore, accept Our Lady and the Gospel seriously, and God will take care of us.

You heard about the rich young man who came back despondent from the meeting with Jesus. Jesus said it is virtually impossible for the rich to enter the Kingdom of God, « It is easier for a camel to go through the eye of a needle, than for a rich man to be saved ». It is true – it is harder for a drunkard to give up alcohol than for him to go through the eye of a needle; he who is imbued with materialism does not perceive any other reality; in fact, after a certain time, not only will he not see it, but he will not have any desire to go to Paradise.

A friend of mine who studied theology and is now a psychiatrist in Rome visited one day a street-walker and asked her, « Do you want to confess? ». She replied, « As you wish », but was not really willing to. My friend then asked her, « Do you not wish to go to Paradise? ». She said, « No, I do not, because one can only find the poor and miserable there ». « Are you afraid of going to hell? ». She replied, « No, I am not, because there one can find the rich and enjoy oneself ».

So there, you see the consequences of life. A person is not capable of seeing or deciding anymore.

When Jesus says, «How difficult for a rich man to enter the Kingdom of God», we must consider how rich in pleasures we are in the West and how far too little room we have found for God and the spirit.

Let us also consider the words of the Author of Wisdom, saying, «I have loved it more than light, more than health, more than power, more than kings' thrones».

If you seriously accept Ivanka's experience, who hugged her mother who had died four and a half years ago, if you are aware of eternal life, then everything changes in your lives. Then following God is no longer difficult – on the contrary, we are not interested in what destroys us any more, but rather, in what brings us to eternal enjoyment, to peace, to the union with God.

Looking at Fatima's prophecies and at what the visionaries are saying these days, we can say that we are already in a decisive period of time and that these very ugly events are awaiting us. We must take what Our Lady says seriously.

Do also take your inner path seriously. Earlier on Our Lady was saying, «*Go to confession once a month*». She then said, «*Once a week*», referring mostly to young people. She is now saying, «*Confess even the smallest sins, because when you go to meet God you will suffer for having just one sin inside you*».

And I am telling you, from experience, we must ponder a lot on the Gospel and pray a lot in order to be able to see our sins, since we have lived through a period virtually without God, when Christians and unbelievers were similar. We have absorbed many ideas and many things and behave like the atheists do. Now, therefore, in what do Christians and unbelievers differ?

Ask yourselves how much of your day do you devote to prayer. And in prayer, do you rest in God, are you happy, or do you really have to fight in order to be a bit recollected? If we are totally distracted and have to work so hard to enter prayer, then we are very far from God, perhaps because of our personal sins, but certainly for those collective ones...

We are far from God, but you all know well enough what is of interest to you.

When one is in love he is totally open to the other person, he desires her always. When you are about to discover a major gain, you do not have to struggle to think and be concentrated on that gain, but instead, you will always have your mind and heart there, with that money, with those riches, with that beauty.

If we do not accept God seriously, and consequently, not even eternal life, it will be very difficult for us to pray, to fast, to give up small things. That is why I am asking you to accept God seriously, to accept Our Lady seriously.

There is a temptation amongst pilgrims of a certain hesitancy, « Let us wait and see... ». We shall see nothing that way.

If a boy goes to school and says, « Let us wait and see, let us see what is going to happen », before he even starts, he will never finish his schooling.

There is then another temptation, a confusion in the minds and hearts : « We must wait for the Church's definition », and one hears no end of talk.

It is satan who prefers darkness and does not want clear ideas.

But I am asking you to follow the simple road of conversion, of prayer, of fasting – it has been the safest road from the beginning, since the time Jesus founded the Church up to the present day. Our Lady's message tells us the same thing.

If you set yourselves to practise these messages in earnest the light will increase in your hearts and you will not allow satan to bring about attacks of hesitancy or confusion, not even of misinformation.

We have also noticed some lies in several Italian newspapers; we have written to them in order to have such misinformation corrected, but they refused.

Therefore, just follow the inner path of the messages and they will bring you to the light.

Many of you have come here asking for some graces. I ask you – please, do look first of all for a deep confession, that confession which may mark the beginning or the continuation of a conversion. Yesterday, at the beginning of Mass there was a cry, « From the depths, to you I cry out, O Lord ».

If we recognise our sins, we must carry on crying out in order to be freed from such sins. If we confess to the priest, « I have done this, I have done that », and continue to live as we have done so far, it is just useless.

Confession must be the start of conversion or the continuation of the same. Without this, the Sacrament of penance will not bear any fruit.

So then, do not go asking the visionaries for answers to your problems. The visionaries cannot give you such answers; it is the Holy Spirit who will give you the answers. You can see that Our Lady Herself does not give final answers, but only indicative ones. Have faith, fast, pray – then we ourselves will be the ones to reach the light, to reach the inner answer of the heart.

He who comes here to receive an answer will go back home without being healed.

On your way back to Italy, you must continue your pilgrimage towards the light of the Holy Spirit which will be granted unto you through conversion, through prayer.

Then you will obtain the sure answer.

Then I want to tell you – carry on praying. How much? Until you feel full, until you feel the peace, the joy, the certainty of being able to spend a day with God and in God. One eats several times a day in order to gain strength and similarly let us also pray this way. Carry on deepening your prayer.

People often say, « How does one pray? ». The same as you would speak to another person. You look at her face, you listen, you talk, you ask questions...

Open the Gospel and look at God's face as expressed in the Gospel. You have heard Him, you have looked at Him a thousand times. Start talking, crying out, praising, asking, listening to what the Lord says, carry on being friends with God.

Unfortunately, if we have to be taught how to pray, it means that we are still children in faith, that we have forgotten to be with Jesus, to live with Jesus. Therefore, get down to praying, deepening your prayer. As you open yourselves to prayer, graces will reach you and you will not bother about your ailments, your troubles.

There is another thing I want to tell you and that is – offer your ailments to the Lord, offer your crosses to the Lord at anytime, but at this moment most especially.

Besides prayer, Jesus is looking for people willing to offer sacrifices spontaneously. Offer your sacrifices and your crosses and you will be rewarded a hundred times as much. If you take care of the Lord, He will take care of you.

(Fr. Tomislav Vlašić - 14 October 1985)

« The only attitude of the Christian towards the future is hope »

I greet you. Welcome. My wish is that you may really receive the graces God is offering you in this sanctuary. For us priests, it is always rather difficult when pilgrims come – there are people coming for the first time, others who have been several times. some immersed in prayer, others who have to start all over again. It is therefore difficult for us to talk to people.

I shall try and keep everyone happy. Our Lady is continuing to invite people to conversion, prayer, fasting; every Thursday there is a message for the Parish and for those who wish to listen to these messages.

In the messages given every Thursday, do not look for a theology, for a lesson, but for a call. Our Lady invites, admonishes, calls. urges us on so that we may grow in conversion.

I am now going to share a thought with you.

Yesterday I told the Italian pilgrims – accept Our Lady and all these events seriously and do not expect anything; live the messages. This evening I want to begin from this plea by adding – accept Our Lady and Her apparitions seriously. It is not something private, but is is a message for the whole of mankind. Doctors have worked hard enough at it and, up to now, we do not know whether ecstasies such as these have ever been examined in the whole of the Church's history; doctors say it is either a supernatural fact or a preternatural one, they cannot explain it in a natural way.

On the other hand, messages such as peace, conversion, prayer. fasting are key messages, without which we are unable to face the future of the world. This evening I want to say to all of you – walk in hope, live hope. I want to help you a little so that you may discover hope.

Many people who come here open themselves too little to hope, and instead of being open to God, they are open to themselves alone, instead of being open to God's plans, they shut themselves in. Many come only with their own plans for their health, to solve their problems, they come with fears and go back with fears; they do not get changed and cannot, therefore, live hope. One of the problems I have come across with the pilgrims, particularly in confession, has been a worry about the world's future. We must be realistic in looking at the future, with regard to both our earthly and our spiritual life.

Our Lady addressed Herself to us Christians by saying through young Jelena, « *The only attitude of the Christian towards the future is hope* ». Another time She said that when we ponder on evil, we are on the road towards it and has invited us to live peace, to think peace.

It is very important now for us to look towards the future with hope, but we shall have hope only to the degree in which we give up selfishness, egocentrism, this earthly life, and turn towards the supernatural life.

I hope I do not have to explain this theme to you. It is sufficiently outlined in last Sunday's liturgy, where that young man, in order to achieve the perfect life, had to forsake all his riches, indeed all his riches, to go further in his perfect life. And the first reading told us that we must love wisdom more than health, more than light, more than power.

Now, if we want to discover hope, we must be totally open to God, and we will be able to be open to God when we really place our hope in eternal life. This is the reality of the Eucharist – the death and resurrection of Jesus Christ.

As long as we are people only caring about our earthly problems, from that very moment, we will be people with inner fear, because we want to keep something for ourselves.

When we become people totally abandoned to God and heavenly life, then we are people of hope.

What does living hope mean at the moment? I have noticed this – we Christians, we analyse the world the same way as atheists do and every day are forever moaning; we are therefore nourished with disappointment, with something which does not give hope. If we Christians cannot go further, if we, at this moment are incapable of finding hope and of announcing it to others, then we have failed our task, we have not practised it. The kind of hope God is offering us in this place is an opening towards the heavenly light, it is an opening through which the world can be saved; whereas with human means it will not be saved, neither here on earth, nor in Heaven. Our Lady has come as a sign in order to open us up towards the reality of Heaven.

During this period I have experienced in my soul how difficult it is to live hope.

I will give you just one of my experiences – one evening I felt like crying when I discovered I had failed. As I examined my conscience I found no mortal sins, as they say, but I discovered I had totally failed. During the day I had met some priests, some friends; I did not say anything against anybody and I spent some time with them. They began analysing the world, the Church; they began to find so many difficulties and spent hours on end doing so, yet I had no strength to enlighten them, to drive them forward; I did not have the strength to say to them, « My dear brother priests, we have been talking in vain for one, two hours; it would have been better to get down to prayer in order to search for light, to help the Church, to help the world ». That day I realised I had wasted a lot of time instead of living hope, of being hope for my brethren, for all those who were complaining and finding no end of difficulties, of sins, of problems. We cannot achieve hope without prayer. That is the way Our Lady has been guiding people in prayer during all this time, that they might meet God and the light of the Holy Spirit in their hearts, and then be able to bring hope to the world. I believe that, without prayer, we are unable to discover hope. If we analyse the life of a saint we notice that as he progressed in his spiritual life and prayer life, hope became the light and the reality of the saint. With prayer we go beyond human hope, we depend on God.

My deep experience is this – my words as a priest are always empty without prayer, they mean nothing or too little. I have never had problems with my sermon – after a long prayer, words would come from the heart.

Our Lady has invited us to peace, to hope; along this path She has been continuously inviting us, « *Pray, pray, pray* ». Several times She told little Jelena, « *I have nothing else to tell you but – Pray, pray, pray* ».

Yesterday some people were asking me how to pray and if I would teach them to pray. I told them that it is easy, one must just decide to start praying.

The same way we know how to talk to a friend for hours and hours, similarly it is only natural to talk to Jesus Christ.

Take up the rosary, pray the Our Father, but think of what you are saying to God. Think over what you are saying to God. Open the Gospel and listen to what God has to say to you. If you do this, it is a continuous conversation with Jesus Christ.

One must pray a lot, one must pray a great deal.

Why must one pray a great deal? Do you know why? Why do we all complain – I am absent-minded, I cannot be recollected?

We are not absent-minded when it comes to gaining something; when we like something or a person, then we are united with it. We are absent-minded because we are far from God, because we do not sufficiently look for God, because we have devoted too much time to the world and too little time to God.

I therefore invite you to continuous prayer, to a continuous deepening of prayer – the light of the Holy Spirit will enlighten you and you will be the people of hope.

What you see to-day, we shall see tomorrow with greater clearness; what you did not see yesterday, you shall see in a month's time with inner eyes, if you carry on praying and pondering on what God has told you or what Our Lady is telling you. In order to live this opening in prayer, we must, dear brethren, take a step forward, we must deepen our confession. Remember, from the beginning Our Lady has invited you all to conversion and confession. In 1982 She invited us to a monthly confession. However, to the members of the prayer group She recommends weekly confession and, again, to those who live their faith more profoundly She recommends weekly confession, because confession is an instrument given by God, a Sacrament by means of which we deepen our spiritual life. If we practise it once a year, once every five years, we will not reach spiritual depth.

In a message Our Lady said, « *Confess even the smallest sins, for at the moment of the happenings, even a small sin will make you suffer. Purify yourselves* ».

I am following the path of the prayer group and I must tell you that Our Lady is striving – so to speak – to continuously purify the group more and more and the members of the group, and, as this inner purification occurs so does the hope I have been telling you about increase.

I beg you once again – live hope, do not go back home all concerned with your problems, but concerned with God's plan. Do not go back home carrying your fears of the future, but joy, peace, confidence towards the future, since God opens the doors of Paradise if we are ready to follow Him.

Only if we will be people of peace, hope, then will we be able to bring Our Lady's messages to the world.

One thing connected with this I want to emphasise – when in Medjugorje, first of all start praying, going to confession which will mark the beginning of conversion, or a continuation of conversion.

Do not let the visionaries be the main object for you; do not try and be present at the time of the apparitions. Remember, Our Lady once said, « *It is better to stay in church praying than to stay near the visionaries out of curiosity during the apparitions* ».

It is for this reason that the priests do not allow anybody in the room during the apparitions. It is better for everyone to stay open hearted, praying, in order to receive the inner light, rather than watching from the outside.

(Fr. Tomislav Vlašić - 15 October 1985)

In this period God and Our Lady want people who are ready to offer everything

Welcome. I really wish that you may receive all the graces God and Our Lady are offering you here.

... When I see you pilgrims, a majority of you prefers to listen with your ears, rather than with your hearts. But I do beg you to set about listening with your hearts.

One can only listen with one's heart if one is immersed in prayer, if there really is total abandonment to God, if we have time to pray, it we do not to listen to the visionaries, but listen to the voice of the Holy Spirit within us. When I say this, it is important to know that Our Lady does not speak only to the visionaries, but also to each of us, although in a different way.

In a message of 1984 Our Lady told the prayer group, through Jelena, that in every prayer one must listen to God's voice, one must try and understand it. If we, therefore, pray this way and, after prayer, we have not seen anybody, we have not heard anybody, then most probably our prayer was not genuine.

If prayer is – as it must be – the dialogue with God, then we must look at Him with our souls, we must listen to Him, we must be in tune with Him, with His Word, with His messages.

Please acquire an attitude of inner listening; I am telling you this, as otherwise, you will not understand Medjugorje.

You would like to listen to the messages and the explanation of what is happening here; I cannot tell you what is going on whilst your hearts are closed.

Now, when thinking of Medjugorje, they all think of the six visionaries – that is not enough. When I now look at Medjugorje, visionaries are for me just one of the signs of Our Lady's presence here, but there are other various deeper gifts in and around Medjugorje, and connected with Medjugorje all over the world.

Many gifts are still hidden, many people are still hidden, but are growing. God is preparing them for the future events.

This you will never understand unless you acquire an inner listening, unless you pray with your hearts, unless you are totally abandoned to God.

Moreover, those amongst you who pray in groups according to Our Lady's intentions will not discover the gifts until you have started listening with your hearts. Many people come and ask me how they can form a prayer group, but the actual formation of a prayer group in its exterior structure is not important; what is important is an inner opening to God, an inner path. The groups guided by Our Lady here in Medjugorje are different from other groups, only because here we can hear Our Lady's voice guiding the groups and not because the girls and boys are any different from the others. The difference between them and the others consists only in the fact that Our Lady's voice can be heard, and Our Lady simply explains the steps to be taken.

If you want to form prayer groups, seek first of all to bring people to prayer, to a desire to reach out for God and to live Our Lady's messages; the Holy Spirit will give you the words and you will be enlightened as to how to go ahead. I cannot tell you how to go ahead with a group.

There are several groups here as well as sub-groups. Both last month and this month I have joined several small groups in prayer and we have realised that there is no need for a programme for prayer; sometimes we have been praying for hours without a programme, just staying with God, since for him who loves God, for him who believes in God with all his heart, when his heart is opened, there is always something to say, to sing, to exchange with God, to listen to...

Prayer and the formation of prayer groups depends on inner formation and, as a group progresses in spiritual life, the Holy Spirit enlightens its people as to how they can walk, go forward. It is important to emphasize that prayer groups are not made up according to human techniques, but according to God's will.

If prayer groups are formed with an attitude of meeting God, of living God, of living God's Word, then it will be the Holy Spirit to guide them through those responsible; light will be given; it is God who will take care of them.

In order to reach this inner listening – in the messages given to the prayer groups in the last few months – there is another typical message, besides prayer, which was given also to the Parish before the feast of the Exaltation of the Cross – i.e. to be consecrated to the Cross.

In several messages Our Lady has been looking for people prepared to sacrifice their lives to God; She has been looking for people ready to offer everything to God, so that, through their sufferings, the world and the souls may be saved.

Do not forget – when you are ready to offer your lives, to offer everything, then you are ready to pray, then the opening of the heart takes place.

Remember the Gospel of the Sunday before last – that young man placed himself before Jesus and asked Him what he had to do in order to achieve eternal life. Jesus replied that he had to follow the commandments. But the man wanted his life to be perfect and so Jesus told him to forsake everything. The Gospel says that he was rich and he left in sadness, but Jesus too, was sad.

We must understand that if we wish to be completely ready at God's service, we must make voluntary sacrifices.

When I heard this message, I started purifying my room by removing from it all superfluous things and it took me about a week to do so. I have not yet managed to get rid of many of the superfluous things, but I am still in the process of emptying my room of useless things. Start emptying yourselves as well in this period and you will see how much time you have to spare, how much time is used up in a superfluous way, how much time you tend to spend in front of the television, how many hours are spent uselessly, how many things are in your rooms, in your houses, while people are dying of starvation.

All this is important to notice, for when we will have emptied our lives of all superfluous things, of all our needs, then we shall be able to go forward, like that young man who was called to a perfect life.

It is most important – I would say mainly for priests – to return to those spiritual exercises done at the time when people were seeking penance entirely of their own will, when they were seeking sacrifices to offer God. It seems to me that, at this moment in history, we have forgotten those sacrifices, so much so that educational teaching does not know sacrifices. They say sacrifices have to be avoided or removed, instead of them being accepted with good will and offered to God entirely of one's own free will in order to save others.

In this period, God and Our Lady want people who are ready to offer everything. However, he who has decided to offer everything must beware of two things: Firstly, he must repeat the offer every day and during his life seek those sacrifices to offer to God; secondly, he must make sure if he really has consecrated himself as a victim, he must be aware of the fact that Jesus is seriously accepting this consecration and already starting to make plans for him.

After this he must make sure he does not escape from those crosses Our Lord will give him. You must, however, be conscious of the fact that, for all the crosses Our Lord gives you, you will be rewarded a hundred times, here on earth itself with blessedness of the heart.

If you so live your future you will bring no fear of chastisements, of difficulties; your only aim will be to meet Jesus, to meet God, to be united with Him and live for the whole of eternity.

To end, I would like to emphasize that you must listen with your hearts and not with your ears; in order to enter the depth of prayer you must sacrifice your own selves, you must sacrifice yourselves and offer yourselves as victims to God. With the offer we make God, we become more open to listening to Our Lord's and Our Lady's messages.

(Fr. Tomislav Vlašić - 16 October 1985)

« Everything has its time »

Belgrade Television has shown a documentery film on Medjugorje. When one already knows the situation from the beginning, this event appears even greater than it did at first sight. It is the first time someone has spoken in this manner – it is a documentary of about an hour, a really good one, followed by discussion. But how can sociologists, psychologists, neuropsychiatrists debate on these things if they do not believe in God? They had a debate; there was also a representative of the Orthodox Church and he was the best of them all, as he gave some very good explanations regarding faith, mystery, the visions, the apparitions and did not fall short on other issues either.

He told a psychologist, « Can a person who is colour-blind give his judgement on colours? ». That is, in other words, how can an unbeliever talk about the apparitions? Surely, he must always explain them on a pathological, psychological or sociological level, but never on a spiritual one.

There was also a representative of the Catholic Church, an actual member of the Commission and with regard to him I will say in a nutshell – when he had to speak, he did not, and when he did, he spoke badly.

However, on the whole it was something very positive.

Marija Pavlović spoke in such an inspired way that I said that, had they all spoken against the apparitions, Marija would have amazed everyone, for she was so genuine and said some really good things. It is quite clear, therefore, that this is not the hour of triumph for us, but just a new appeal, a new call to be accepted, in order to believe in and live the messages.

In the last message Our Lady asks us to take care of our hearts, to clean up every corner of our hearts. She said, « *Now that your work on the land is over you have more time available. You clean every corner of your homes, but neglect your hearts* ».

And so She invited us to clean our hearts.

It is very important to feel that everything has its own time, that we are invited to find a daily balance – the balance of our time spent, that is, finding time for prayer, for spiritual life, the same way one finds time for work, study, rest.

Our Lady proposed we should pray – When one prays well, I believe that an hour and a half is sufficient. If one were also to manage to go to Mass sometimes, perhaps that too, would give some balance to our day.

You see, even when one goes to work or to study one does not go out without having washed oneself; it takes some time to wash one's face, to shave; women especially need more time in the morning. And that is all right, it would not be right to go out anyhow; it is not normal.

We must ask ourselves, however, how long we devote to prayer in the morning.

If we say, « I have no time », is it that we seem to have time for breakfast, for other things, but not for prayer? We go out with a starving soul, with a soul which has had nothing to eat all morning. How can we face the day? How can we meet others? How can we give peace? How can we forgive? Be reconciled? An empty soul, an empty heart cannot forgive, an empty soul is amidst conflicts; there is a saying here, « If one does not eat bread, one must eat bones ».

So, you see, if Our Lady says, « *Everything has its time* », one ought to find time in the morning for prayer, for one's soul.

One ought to find time for prayer in the evening also. And in a message Our Lady has asked us to become active in prayer.

Our Lady says, « *Everything has its time* »: this message is very important for parents. You must know that everything has its time, but if you do not know it, how can the young know it? How can the children? If you start immediately, if you start from scratch, it will not be difficult even for the young, even for the children to learn about this time.

... Why does Our Lady ask for prayer? Prayer is a means of obtaining peace, joy, of being able to be reconciled. We all want peace, we all want reconciliation, to be loved and to love, but it is quite something else if we all desire the means to receive this grace.

I will give you an example – surely, at school every student wants to succeed at the end of the school year; this is certain, but it does not follow that all students want to study. The same goes for all of us – we all want peace, reconciliation, love, but we do not all wish to take up the means to receive it, which is prayer.

Two Dutch girls left their testimony with me: « We have discovered that prayer is the path to peace and to happiness and to joy. And this means a lot, because after having discovered this we were able to stop smoking hashish, drinking, and other things ». This is the way to peace. We cannot give up nothing. I am certain that only when we have discovered the finer things, when we have discovered a greater value, can we then forsake the other things.

And so, if any of you is still saying, « I cannot resist swear words », I think he is saying so because he has not yet discovered prayer, the joy of prayer. If someone says he cannot give up alcohol or other things he knows are not good, I believe that it is only because he has not yet discovered what these girls say – the joy, the happiness in prayer.

I want to repeat what Our Lady said, « *I am saved, but I want you too, to be saved* ». And one cannot be saved in this world unless one starts with prayer, with fasting, with this kind of faith. In a message Our Lady is inviting us to be consecrated to the Cross – that means, being with the Cross, feeling the Cross, talking to the Cross, letting it speak. What is the Cross talking about? « Here is your son, here is your Mother ». The Cross talks about forgiveness, sacrifice, love and eternal life. If we, in our homes, carry on swearing, doing evil before the Cross, if we behave selfishly before the Cross, we can effectively say the Cross does not speak anymore, it is dumb.

But the Cross wants to talk to us, Our Lady wants the Cross to talk to us. Be consecrated, open your hearts and you will see that it will tell you – perhaps as with St. Francis – it will say, « Go and renew your life, your family, your love, your parish, your church, your community ».

Do not say, « I cannot », for the Lord knows what He is saying and when He invites us to something, He also gives us the graces, He also gives us the strength.

We can do nothing with our own strength, but as we open ourselves in prayer, in fasting, we are given the same experience as St. Paul had, when he said, « I am a weak man, but in my very weakness I have lived, I have experienced the glory of the Cross, the strength of Grace ».

(Fr. Slavko Barbarić - 18 October 1985)

If we put ourselves at God's disposal, it is God who leads us

I greet you, I do not have much time, I cannot stay long.

I have been talking to you far too much these days, have I not? When words fill up too much space in one's heart, then they leave no room for spiritual creativity; that is why I say to you, I have spoken far too much!

I only want you to go forward, to carry on, since every word of God, every word of Our Lady increases the graces. Do not worry as to how to form a group, do not worry as to how to pray, but above all, start praying, conversing with God, with Jesus.

For example, people usually say that the Rosary is no meditative prayer, that it is no contemplative prayer. It is too rational, one cannot manage to pray it with one's heart; but in these days I have been in contact with some people who are concerned with deep meditation, where there is silence; indeed, they had a problem with words as they needed total silence, without prayers, to pray with silence.

During the two or three days of their stay in Medjugorje they have meditated a lot and felt a real need to pray the Rosary. They needed to say a thousand Hail Mary's, to invoke « Hail Mary » all the time.

In that prayer there was no impediment to entering into depth; on the contrary, they were opening themselves more and more, as they prayed. So you see that it does not depend on the form of prayer but on our hearts, on their opening. At the bottom of prayer there is always a desire to reach out for God, to find God, to live what God wants. So therefore, if we put ourselves at God's disposal, it is God who is leading us along different paths.

Let us not worry on the spiritual level either, this principle is valid for the material level as for the spiritual one. If we remain worried people at a spiritual level we are prevented from going ahead.

Recently I met a mystical person who has supernatural visions and who told me that what makes Jesus sad is indeed our carrying fear within ourselves. He is just, but He is also merciful. He would rather die again than lose one soul.

You see how we must dismiss any worry. There should be – inside our hearts – a continuous chant to God's mercy, we ought to have God's mercy actually singing inside us.

And there shall we also find humility and everything, when God's mercy flourishes inside us.

So, I wish you to become more and more a praise of God's mercy, a real joy. This way, you will be able to bring the messages to the entire world.

(Fr. Tomislav Vlašić - 18 October 1985)

Our Lady takes new steps everywhere

... Yugoslavian television has transmitted a broadcast on Medjugorje lately. In it, the orthodox priest spoke thus, « This is something great also for Ecumenism, for all these orthodox believers who have already come and for those who will follow ».

This seems to me to be a step taken by Our Lady.

At the same time, in London, an article appeared in a very important paper and we were invited to give a short talk on television. The woman journalist who was in the studio with me gave a very important testimony. The interviewer asked, « So, you have been to Medjugorje, what have you seen? ». She replied, « I am a Protestant, non-practising; my husband too is a non-practising Protestant. Our photographer is Jewish, the interpreter, a girl from Belgrade, orthodox, a psychologist. All four of us were against all this ». And she said in front of all the English audience : « I have not seen Our Lady, but I can honestly say that all four of us have changed. We have changed our way of thinking and I am sure that the visionaries do see someone, but I do not know who that is ».

This is a highly important testimony.

Through these events Our Lady takes new steps in every direction. This surely, is not the moment of triumph of something, but it means for us yet another obligation to take what is happening seriously.

(Fr. Slavko Barbarić - 19 October 1985)

« If you were to accept my love, you would never sin »

I greet you. Welcome.

Instead of starting to talk to you, I invite you to pray the first joyful mystery together, so that our hearts may be open to God's messages, in the same way the Virgin's heart was, and may the Holy Spirit descend on us, as He descended upon the Virgin...

Regina Pacis, ora pro nobis.

A few days ago young Jelena told us that, for three consecutive evenings, Our Lady repeated the message, « *If you were to accept my love, you would never sin* ».

On the fourth evening the visionary asked, « But why do you repeat the same message? ». Our Lady replied, « *I have nothing else to tell you* », and She cried.

You see, « *If you were to accept my love you would never sin* »; similar messages have been imparted on various occasions, calling people to the opening of hearts, to open oneself totally, in order to receive the love Our Lady is bringing. And if we are in a position to receive this love, then we are also able to accept the light which comes from Heaven, and not to sin.

During this meeting I would rather like to guide you into the depth of the opening of the heart.

When one talks about Medjugorje, one talks about visionaries. In my opinion, and according to my experience, one only tends to see one side, which is the easiest one to see. But there is yet another reality.

After this period of apparitions which started on the 24 June 1981 till now, I must tell you, there is another manifestation occuring in Medjugorje, around Medjugorje and all over the world.

Other people exist who are still unknown, through whom Our Lady and God are carrying out their programme. And when I tell you that the apparitions of Medjugorje are true and I say, « I believe », it is still not enough. What I should tell you is, « I do know », because certain things have come true. It is not a matter of faith anymore, but rather a matter of knowledge, for we have seen and still see the work in progress.

And the other side of it is represented by the very opening of the hearts of those who wish to open themselves to God.

The six visionaries are only − in my opinion − a visible sign to makind; whilst others are people who are invited to open themselves to God and to offer themselves to God, so that God may deepen and fulfill His plan. I see this work being accomplished, for I hear of so many people and groups who have received a particular task during this period. I am telling you this, so that you, too, may be included in God's plan; by means of the apparitions each one of you is invited to live the Gospel thoroughly, in such a way, that each of you may be offered to God and God may − through us all − bring salvation to the whole of mankind.

I would now like to ask each one of you to enter into the divine plan more deeply. With regard to anything new, I cannot tell you anything. Anything I can say cannot possibly satisfy; you will only be satisfied if you open your hearts wide, only if you yourselves will be so fully open to accept the Virgin's love, God's love.

I only want to emphasise one aspect: a person who is living the special gifts in a hidden sort of way because God wants him to grow, told me a few days ago that Jesus is very sad because people do not understand His mercy. People accept Him as a Judge, as a just man, the just God; He is just, but also merciful. People forget that He is ready to die again for each one of us. Jesus is sad because we carry fear within ourselves.

So you see: if we wish to live this reality of the apparitions, we must all enter into the full depth of our lives.

It is easy to say, « I believe in God, I believe in the apparitions, I believe in the Gospel ». But it is difficult to enter the full depth of one's own heart and cast out all fear, every worry, all tension.

If we want to achieve the knowledge of the Gospel, the knowledge which enlightens us totally, which gives us new life, we must enter the full depth of our hearts.

I shall read you what we read this morning for the Mass of St. Peter of Alcantara, a Franciscan Friar who lived a life of penance in accordance with the Gospel.

We read two texts, Chapter III of the letter to the Philippians, where it says – amongst other things – « All these things were a gain for me. I instead, valued them as a loss for the Love of God. Actually, I consider everything a loss in comparison with the supreme advantage of Jesus Christ, my Lord, for whom I have deprived myself of everything and I have valued everything as garbage with a view to gaining Christ, finding myself once again in Him, not with my own justice which stems from the law, but with the one obtainable by the faith in Christ, justice which comes from God and rests in faith ».

Moreover, we have read the Gospel of St. Luke, where it says, « Do not worry for your lives, for what you shall eat, for what you shall wear, for life is worth more than nourishment and the body more than your dress ».

It is vital to continue this reading with an opening of heart – God wants to unburden us of our problems, of our worries, and He goes right to the end of redemption.

We must remove all fear, every worry from ourselves.

I must stress the fact that it is not a question of worries as to what to eat, drink or wear but, – in people who have offered themselves to God – the greatest worry is the spiritual one – the worry of saving others, the worry of saving ourselves; not even at a spiritual level should there be worry within us. We can be occupied, not preoccupied.

In this sense, Jesus stresses the fact that we must be like a blossoming flower, growing without tension, without cares – all comes from God.

Therefore, if we are able to live the reality of a flower, of a bird, we shall be able to have a life as God wants, we shall be able to proclaim the Gospel. This is important. Let us go a few days back in time to the feast of St. Margaret Mary Alacoque. In her writings, she says, « From Jesus' heart three currents of grace arise : the first one gives us contrition, deep repentance; the second one is the one of love, indeed for those who place themselves at God's disposal in order to announce His works, and the third one carries love and peace for those who want to be perfect in God ». This mystic emphasises the very gift of peace, saying, « Pray for peace, in order to have it, in order to keep it ». So if you look at the Gospel you will see how Jesus leads us to this peace, not to be worried, not for us to be free from worries, but for us to be rooted in God. It is God who provides us with everything.

If we start living this reality, a total abandonment to God, a total abandonment to the Virgin, then we are left only with inner peace from which the immense joy, the love and the redeemed life God is giving us derive.

If you want to live Our Lady's messages, I say to you – you must enter into deep prayer every day.

I will give you my own experience – today I got up at five thirty. After having washed, I started thanking God for the day and at six o'clock I immediately settled down to an inner abandonment in order to prepare myself for the day. At a quarter to seven (forty minutes – during which I was preparing myself interiorly in prayer of abandonment) I went to pray the third part of the Rosary together with the people. And I felt how the Rosary maintains a certain recollection in the heart.

I celebrated Mass and after Mass, regretted not having got up even earlier, because I felt I had had too little time to devote to deepening my spiritual life.

We cannot enter into the depth of the Gospel if our prayer life is a rush, if it is hurried.

One can pray in a hurry only if one has been able to reach peace as a consequence of longer and deeper previous times of prayer. And now another testimony. The day before yesterday I had a meeting with a small group of Italians – people particularly devoted to God and to the Virgin. And yet, these very people could not pray – they could not understand the Rosary. It seemed like empty words, they could not undertsand why one should repeat « Hail Mary »; they were inclined rather towards silent, meditative prayer in which they would place themselves before God in silence.

After having spent two successive nights in prayer, the day before yesterday they came to me to tell me, « We need to repeat a thousand Hail Mary's, to repeat the Hail Mary all the time ».

It would appear that their hearts had been transformed in a new sweetness of admiration: « Hail Mary full of grace, blessed are thou amongst women... »: a yearning, an inner cry, a sweetness and then the invitation to help mankind, all of us.

Therefore, from this example, you can see how the problem of spiritual life does not lie in forms; it is rather the opening of our hearts. It is in this dedication to God. If we come to a total opening of our hearts then forms become immaterial; we will find them.

Therefore, do not ask me – how shall one form a prayer group? It is like a woman asking – how shall I give birth to my child? Everything comes from life, from God.

I will give you yet another piece of evidence. When I found myself with a small group I led with particular care, we started praying without a plan. We dwelt upon prayer for several hours regardless of a plan – we started talking to God, exchanging experiences, asking, listening, singing like we would with friends. Our hearts are the starting point of our spiritual life, for our life of faith.

I want to refer back to what I was saying earlier, when stating that there are two aspects to Medjugorje, two sides of the apparitions – the six visionaries, representing the visible moment of the apparition, and the opening of the faithful through which God is revealing Himself more and more.

And my wish is that each of you together with me, may become more and more open, through whom God reveals Himself and brings the messages of salvation to mankind. Our Lady can speak through the life of each one of us, provided that each one of us is a child born of the apparitions, of the Virgin Herself.

How can we open our hearts to the Lord?

Our Lady showed us the way – prayer, fasting. We must – in my opinion – open our hearts by devoting time to God, by searching for God.

Our problem is this – we do not search for God.

People complain, « I cannot be recollected... ». It is a natural consequence of our unbelief. If I devote twenty-four hours to material things and, perhaps five minutes to God, I cannot be recollected since my heart is lost in human possessions. I think, I ponder, I make plans on a material level.

The same thing happens in the life of a football player if he does not train every day; if he does not live in constant training, he is not in a position to play.

Even the cleverest of football players cannot play a match if they are not ready, if they are not in constant training.

We must, in our lives renounce many a thing – the things I have at my disposal are my hindrance, they are the source of my worry. I must remove all that prevents me from being with God, in God. We must therefore be very poor – in the likeness of St. Francis, who removed even his clothes to give them back to his father. « Now I am free to say: Our Father who art in heaven ». When we are stripped of everything and God becomes the only desire there is in our hearts, then it is easy to enter into prayer and be recollected.

... Are silence and listening already prayer before God?

There is an empty kind of silence and the silence in which we can meet God. There are depressed people who place themselves in silence, where depression still remains. There are people who go into silence and still carry worries inside. Positive silence must be deprived of worries and sins in order to have a free heart so that God and the divine Word can act in us. Therefore, it is in silence that we live redemption.

The answer, the light, the strength, enlightenment will follow silence. We become filled with God.

This is very important, since I have found that, in many prayer groups, there are several who always keep quiet, they stay in silence, and God cannot come into their lives, for they are full of fears.

Their silence is full of problems, full of selfishness.

Our Lady has been teaching us by saying, « *Enter into prayer: many are those who finish prayer without having entered it* ». And She showed us two steps to be taken – remove any sin, recognise it, repent and offer God all one's problems.

One must free oneself of one's problems: then our hearts become free by the action of the Holy Spirit and the Holy Spirit acts in us.

... From my personal experience I can say that the depth of my relation to God through prayer, meditation and reflection, is in the degree of my daily offering of myself through my work. I have found that, when I do not pray enough I am not nourished deeply enough with hope, peace, love, and my working day is not full. I often act with my own human strength and often give of myself, but not what the Lord wants to offer from within myself. In my opinion, we ought to follow Jesus who used to retire in prayer all night long and acted afterwards.

This morning, before Mass, I felt the need to enter into the spirit of the Mass, to be one with Jesus, to offer Jesus inside me to the Father, and not myself.

And I asked Jesus, « Thank you because both of us are one ». And added, « May you be visible in me and not myself, and thus give joy to the Father to-day ». This seems to me to be the way to enter into Jesus: even though I am involved in other works, let Jesus act inside me.

He who sets out on this path will have an ever increasing need to enter into deep prayer, for every day he will discover how inadequate he is, how far from him Jesus still is, and he will need to get back to Him, to pray to Him so that he may be helped, changed, transformed by Him.

Many say that all work is prayer – in one sense it is, whereas in the other it is a false argument. We say that every word is nourishment for us and, surely, that is so, but we cannot be nourished without lunch or supper. We cannot live on a look from our friend alone and therefore, if we are not nourished with deep prayer, penance and conversion, our day can become empty and deceitful. I believe that, in this period, we are all called to discover prayer and, through prayer, make our work edifying.

... It is useless for me to carry on talking to you more in depth unless your hearts are open. If God leads certain people to a high spirituality, He protects them for a while, so that they may have a chance to mature and then bear fruit.

Lucky are those who are hidden from the Italian pilgrims, because the visionaries are almost worn out.

Once Marija said, « find me a sack, tie me up in it and take me away so that I may have some peace ».

God has his own plans, but we can all reach the light through our own opening. It seems to me we want to listen a lot to what people say and too little to what the Gospel says. It would be most important for us if we were to place ourselves daily before the divine Word, in order to – as Our Lady said – root it in our hearts and live it all day long.

(Fr. Tomislav Vlašić - 19 October 1985)

« You still do not understand my great love, make haste to understand it »

I want to set about reflecting with you on the words of Luke's Gospel, chapter XII which we shall be hearing to-night. « There is a baptism I must receive and how distressed I am until it is accomplished. Do you think I came to bring peace on earth? No, but only division. From now on in a household of five people, three will turn against two and two against three, father against son and son against father, mother against daughter and daughter against mother, mother-in-law against daughter-in-law and daughter-in-law against mother-in-law... ».

During this liturgical period the readings make us think about and understand what Our Lord wants. We have heard the Word of Our Lord, in which Jesus says He has not come to bring peace, but indeed, division. Here in Medjugorje, starting from the first meeting, one hears the message of peace. We must understand the kind of peace Our Lady is telling us of and the one Jesus is talking about.

The peace of the Lord is something very deep indeed. In the priest's sermon yesterday, he talked about an experience of parents here on pilgrimage. They had come to Medjugorje from a faraway country seeking a grace for their son, a boy who was determined to abandon school and walk on the streets like so many young people. In Medjugorje, the parents prayed and found a very deep peace. On their return home they learned of their son's having been expelled from school. They said, « When we saw he had been expelled from school we did not lose our peace in the least: we only looked at each other with a deep peace in our hearts. We left him to God without any resentment on our part and we both carried on praying and living the peace found in Medjugorje. After a few weeks time our son confessed, "Your peace upsets me" and, after a certain time, he came to accept school, another school and left the wrong one ».

The parents discovered that their son had abandoned the wrong school chosen by them but not suitable to him. He took another road and – like them – found peace.

Dear Brethren, we must all make a start towards peace this way. Peace can solve all problems; we live in resentment against one another, in despair, and cannot live with our problems, because God is impeded, He cannot work within ourselves.

We must reach the peace of the Lord; but what is this peace? It is not pacifism, it is not the consequence of training techniques, not of yoga techniques. Yoga techniques can lead to silence, tranquility, but cannot lead to the peace of Christ.

When the visionaries describe Our Lady's face and Her behaviour, they describe it not like a peace due to concentration, but like a rose which is opening itself.

Peace is, at the same time, life, dynamics, joy.

Jesus brought peace to his Apostles after His death, the peace which has won everything. So, I invite you to live peace, but you must change your path if you want to have peace. Many people, most of us, want calmness and not peace.

We come to Medjugorje asking Our Lady, « Heal my son, so that I may have calm », « Solve certain problems, so that I may live better on this earth », « Give me a job », « Drive these troubles away... ».

We wish to be calm and we are often like the Apostles waiting for the Kingdom of God for us, for the Kingdom here on earth, for a messianism, and yet we know that that Kingdom the Apostles were waiting for has failed. After death the risen Jesus met them and showed them the way towards peace, « You yourselves must die with me. You yourselves must offer yourselves for me. You must be prepared to die like me. I too, have died ».

Look at what Jesus said to St. Peter, coming to a conclusion, « Truly, truly I say to you – when you were younger you used to gird yourself and go where you wanted to, but when you are old you will stretch out your hands and another will gird your robe and carry you where you do not wish to go ». This he said to show by what death he was to glorify God. And having said this, He added, « Follow me ».

Dear Brethren, if you want to reach the peace the Lord is talking about, you must live today's Gospel, where Jesus said, « I have come to bring fire to this earth, not peace, but division ». He means this – to-day you must be awoken; you are called to make a decision to belong totally to God. And you know Jesus' wish ,« Love God with all your strength, all your heart and love your neighbour like yourselves ».

Do not come to Medjugorje looking for something for yourselves – what we are usually looking for is life on earth. Our Lord said, « Look first of all for the Kingdom of God and all the rest will be granted unto you ».

An illness is not to be cured unless the source of illness is removed. You cannot live in joy, happiness until you have received Jesus Christ, His word, and the same goes for Our Lady's words. If you are able to abandon yourselves totally to Our Lady and God, to offer yourselves to God, then you will find the joy of peace. This is why I told you – the peace Our Lady is talking about is not calmness, pacificism, concentration. It is the kind of peace which cannot be obtained from the world, but only from Jesus Christ. On Tuesday, in a message to the group, Our Lady said, « *You still do not understand the great love I am giving you, make haste to understand it. When I will have finished my apparitions it may be too late for you to understand it* ».

We must really make haste and understand Our Lady's messages. If you wish to make haste, follow today's Gospel.

Talking to several priests, nuns and laymen who were saying, « We believe in the apparitions of Medjugorje », I saw them like the Jews of Egypt, when God said to Moses, « I know they will not listen to you on account of the burdens they are bearing ». I have in this way understood that the people who were telling me « I believe in Medjugorje » were in fact deaf, oppressed by various difficulties, and, at the same time, not hungry for hope. They say,

« Yes, Our Lady said, but... » and from that "but" everything escapes.

A nun said, « I could gather up ten coaches of young people to bring to Medjugorje, but you know how difficult it is; what would they say... ».

Hope is crushed inside us.

If you really want to accept Jesus this evening, accept His words – if we accept him out of our own free will, He is like the fire of love which converts us. If we go through the fire of purgatory it will be difficult, but if we go to hell, as seen by the visionaries, poor us!

Let us accept the fire of love and let us be people determined to follow Christ, to follow Our Lady.

If someone were to be perplexed about the apparitions, let him wonder, « Do I believe in God? Do I believe in Jesus Christ? ». Let him accept the words of the Lord said during this Mass and he will understand Our Lady as well.

Simply dear brethren, I invite you to pray every day – take this up this evening as your programme.

(Fr. Tomislav Vlašić - 24 October 1985)

The task of us Christians is to live hope and peace

In Her message, yesterday, Our Lady said that day by day She wants to clothe us with goodness, divine love and prepare us to become every day more true and ready for the coming of the Lord; hence She was inviting us to accept the messages and live them.

To-day, Mirjana had an apparition of Our Lady lasting eight minutes. We do not know the content. Fr. Pero, who was present, merely told me, « I saw tears in Mirjana's eyes ». The meetings with Our Lady contain some explanation of the secrets, since this visionary has received the task of warning the priest on the first secrets who will in turn warn the world.

In the light of the messages, I would like to comment on the Gospel of this evening.

Jesus used to say to the crowds, « When you see a cloud rising from the west you say immediately that rain is coming. And so it happens. And when the south easterly wind blows you say it will be hot. And so it happens. Hypocrites – you can judge the aspect of the earth and sky, how is it that you cannot judge this time? And why do you not judge what is right by yourselves? When you go with your adversary before the magistrates make sure, on your way, to come to an agreement with him, so that he may not drag you before the judge and the judge deliver you to the officer who will throw you in prison. I can assure you, you will not be able to come out of it, until you will have paid the last penny ».

There, it would suffice us to ponder on the words the Lord told us, « Hypocrites: you can judge the look of the earth and sky, how come you cannot judge this time? ».

I bring the messages to your attention – last night, Our Lady said that, day by day, She is leading us to prepare us for the coming of the Lord. During the apparitions, the visionaries have told us several times that Our Lady says these apparitions are to be the last ones on earth. These apparitions are long, as never before in the history of the Church. We must discover the reason as to why they are so long. The visionaries say it is because they are the last ones for the whole of mankind, the events are very serious. And we must reflect on and understand the time in which we are living. Jesus himself has told us that we are capable of knowing the time; when we can understand the events of the earth and sky, we must understand the spiritual events, as well.

However, we must do something in order to understand the spiritual events.

I shall try and explain what attitude we are to adopt towards the events which are ahead of us.

When we talk of these events, there are people who get frightened. I will bring you the word of John the Baptist who said, « Brood of vipers, who has taught you to escape the imminent wrath? Get down to deeds worthy of conversion, therefore, and do not start telling yourselves -- we have Abraham as a father ».

We must not get frightened, but we must be converted.

Conversion is an act of hope, fear is an act of desperation and we must have an act of hope.

If you live an act of hope, if you live conversion, ahead of you there can only be joy, a waiting for the Saviour, but if selfishness is within you, then also fear will remain within you. I shall try, therefore, and help you understand those hard words of St. John the Baptist to the people. As I was saying, many people hearing these messages get frightened because they are too worried with this earth. « He who loves has no fear », says St. John, but since we are tied to material things, we want first of all the health of our bodies, we want welfare, we are worried about our jobs, we are worried about prolonging our lives by ten days. Then fear is within us. If we really believe in the living God, in eternal life, if we really have accepted this life on earth as being a transition towards a better life, and if we are totally abandoned to God, then, within ourselves there can only be freedom, peace, from which hope derives.

I have just said that many people get frightened, but there is something worse than fright – there is an unconscious fright. There are people who do not want to hear of such talk, who have hidden their own fear.

A priest said a few days ago, « When I read Our Lady's message given at the end of August not to make too much profit out of the grape harvest, some of my parishoners told me, "Why talk of such things? What has this got to do with faith? We do not want to talk about this" ».

To my mind this is a hidden fear; one third of the world is dying of starvation, one third of the world is dying of too much food and unfortunately, amongst those dying because they eat too much are us Christians, the West.

You see – a message must talk to man, to us Christians. Why does the Christian not even want to hear it? Because his soul is closed. To my mind this is worse than open fright, for a greater fear is hidden in the souls who do not even want to hear the Word of the Lord and reject it, and it will be with great difficulty that these very people will be able to open themselves to the Lord's message.

I call on you to open yourselves to the messages of the Gospel – the rest of the liturgical year will tell us about the last events of mankind.

Our Lady's message of yesterday is the light on the liturgical readings we shall be reading in the next few days.

Something else I would like to stress – many people get frightened, but Jesus does not talk to us to frighten us; nor does Our Lady talk to us to frighten us; but both Jesus and Our Lady want us to be attentive, to be discerning, they want us to get to know the historic moments in order for us to go ahead with light.

Jesus said, « When such things will be about to happen, stand up and raise your heads, for your liberation is close at hand ». The task of us Christians is to live hope and peace. In the spring of 1983 Our Lady told Jelena, « *The only attitude on the part of Christians towards the future is hope* ». In another message, She said, « *One must not even think about adverse things; if you think of adverse things with fear, you are on the path towards them* ». We must be hope, we must be light; if we go along with hope and total abandonment then, within us, there will be peace and no room for fear, not even for fanaticism or prophesying, that is, for those who want to pre-determine the future.

We must be abandoned and live with the Lord day by day, totally open to Him.

If we pilgrims place ourselves at the disposal of God and the Blessed Virgin with this attitude of hope, then we can change the world. If we have come here to gain something for ourselves – our bodily health, some grace for our earthly life, we are mistaken. We must be abandoned in the Lord, ready to come face to face with Him, ready to offer our life, in order to live a better life.

Our Lady wants us to place ourselves seriously before Her, before Her messages, She wants us to accept Her messages in earnest and forsake sin forever; by this means you will be able to live the rest of your life with peace and hope, otherwise you will be left with your fears.

Let us offer our lives to the Lord, to Our Lady, in order to live the freedom of heart, the kind of peace from which hope for the future and eternal life originates.

... You must be aware of the fact that Our Lady is amongst us; if you pray with faith She is amongst us.

To explain this better, some pilgrims from Milan once asked through Jelena the following question: « We have come to you, dear Mother, when will you come to Milan? ». Our Lady replied through the visionary, « *When you open your hearts to me* ».

And therefore Our Lady will come to each one of us when we open our hearts.

Here is another example, to explain this to you. I once received, through the visionary, a task I was supposed to perform for Our Lady and I sought an explanation as to how to do it, how to set about it. I asked a question through Marija and obtained the answer, « *Do not worry, I will help you* ».

I did not hear Her voice, but I have felt Her help. So a vocal answer is not the only answer we can obtain from Our Lady. God and Our Lady are answering us even when no voice can be heard, but we hear the answer in our hearts and it is there that a complete answer takes place.

And so I invite you also this evening to confession. And when I ask you to confession, I mean I invite you to make your confession in the light of what we have been considering.

In order to explain this better – it has happened many times that people coming from far away and wanting to meet me for a special confession, when they actually start talking in the confessional box, they do not say anything about the confession itself, do not bring out their sins, but only their problems. One cannot go on like this; you cannot gain anything. If there are no vines, you cannot have the harvest of the spiritual fruits, you are not in a position to welcome Jesus Christ. Before asking for the solution of your problems, start being reconciled with God and your neighbour. seek God's light, which enlightens both your problems and your sins.

Do not look for a recipe for the solution of your problems, but ask the priest for advice as to what spiritual attitude you should take towards your sins, towards your problems. Before trying to solve your problems, you must look for the right attitude you, as a Christian, must take regarding your problems.

I was telling a group a few days ago, « when talking to you as a group to try to clarify a few things, I can sense that you are deaf ». In fact, after the meeting, so many came asking me the same questions, because they have not been listening. They have not been listening because their minds have been concentrated on their problems; and so, enclosed in their problems, they are unable to listen to the Lord's voice. And many are deaf.

I am therefore calling you to a good and sincere confession, to an attitude whereby you will first of all seek God and his Kingdom and then the rest will be granted to you.

(Fr. Tomislav Vlašić - 25 October 1985)

You will not be able to pray deeply until you offer yourselves up to God

Jesus Christ be praised. May He be always praised.

It is customary for us here to reply, « Jesus and Our Lady be praised ».

I greet you all, I want to be the brother of all movements, of all Christians, of all faithful and of all atheists. I really would like, like St. Francis, to love all creatures.

I shall try this evening to give you the main news concerning recent events followed by a short sermon. Unfortunately, the sermons we priests preach tend often to be only comments on the Word of God; instead of bringing God's Word we often only bring our own – in this way one cannot hear the Word of God and of Our Lady.

You all know that the apparitions started on 24 June 1981; the visionaries were originally six, and amongst those six, there are still four who are continuing with daily apparitions. They are: Vicka, Jakov, Ivan and Marija. Ivanka has not seen Our Lady since 7 May 1985. On 6 May 1985 she received the last secret for mankind, namely the tenth; with that secret, Our Lady has concluded the account of the future of one part of the world.

Since that encounter, Ivanka has not seen Our Lady anymore; however, the desire of praying more has increased in her heart, so that she can now meet Her through prayer.

Since Christmas 1982, Mirjana has not been seeing Our Lady daily anymore. This year Our Lady has appeared to her on 18 March, then on 19 March and again, also yesterday.

Mirjana has also had meetings with Our Lady, during which she has heard Her voice; the visionary lives in an inner tension between what she knows and the sinful state of the world.

Yesterday, she had an apparition lasting eight minutes. This apparition had been announced a month ago. What went on in that apparition? Apart from the usual experience which the visionaries share with Our Lady, that is, the blessing, the greeting of Our Lady, immense joy and peace, the visionary also saw, as in a film, the taking place of the first secret, of the first warning to mankind. Fr. Pero, who was there, said, « I saw her eyes full of tears ». Mirjana says she has asked Our Lady the question, « Will it really come so soon? Does it really have to be so harsh? ».

The visionary was praying and begging Our Lady, saying, « How can God have such a hard heart? ».

Our Lady replied, « *God does not have a hard heart, but look around you at how people live, how people sin...* ». Then the visionary said, Our Lady asked another question, « *Just look at the faithful coming to church: do they really come to meet God, or do they come out of habit?* ».

I spoke to the visionary to-day. She told me this, « You can tell everybody – we are at a time of graces, at a time of Our Lady's call, who wants to lead us to salvation. Mankind is going through some very tough moments, through which a harsh purification will take place. After the sign it will be too late ».

The visionary is saying that mankind will reach a point where there will be a meeting with God, when there will be a manifestation of God and this, she says, will be the period of faith, of conversion and that is why She is inviting us to conversion.

However, when one usually talks of these things, that is, of the announcements made by the visionaries, people become afraid.

This means that we have not discovered faith and the visionary says, « But why are you afraid, when we know what awaits us after this earthly life? It is important to live this life, as this is a transition ».

What the visionary emphasises is a conversion, a purification of the heart, a total opening to God in order to live in God. From her explanation one can see that our future, as well as our present, depends on this purification. With a total opening, with a purified heart, we shall be able to go towards the events with joy, with peace and confidence because we will look forward to the wonderful things God has promised us.

And so, what the visionary emphasises is conversion, prayer, a total abandonment to God, so that we may be, at this moment in time, purified and we may live at the time when God will manifest Himself in a special way.

To these words, I would like to add what Our Lady told Jelena in the summer 1983, « *Accept Me in earnest. When God comes amongst you, He does not come for fun, but to talk about serious matters* ». People often say, « Why does God not change the world's situation? ».

I will reply with the words the visionaries have brought us. God wants to change the world, but we do not want it. For more than four years He has been calling us to a change, to conversion, through the Virgin. He is giving us the means for conversion – prayer, fasting, total abandonment to God, but we do not take it seriously.

What I want to tell you is this – you have come here, so try this evening to live for God, to search for God; do not seek healing, do not seek to solve some earthly problem, that will come after your abandonment to God.

We Christians should be the happiest people, and yet, we are often the poorest. God is offering Himself and we, on our part, look for something for ourselves and not for God, from whom comes all our good and blessings.

So, this evening, look for God, but also for Our Lady.

The thought that has been paramount in my heart since last night is this – we are not aware of how much God has given us through the Blessed Virgin.

Unfortunately, many will become aware when things will come to pass. Never before like today, have I discovered that, through the Virgin, God has given us a maternal care; just as a mother takes care of her children, thus has God sent the Blessed Virgin amidst us in this period so that She can take care of us.

And you well know how much worry there is on the part of a

mother towards her child, how many times she gets up at night to watch over her son – even in sleep she is bound to her child.

If we accept Our Lady, we will overcome the trials of this time with great ease.

I will tell you something else which is very important – when you consider the future, when you consider the troubles of today's world, go towards such troubles with joy, since, through the trials laid before us, God will lead us to a more complete purification, so that we may be purified and also the Church may be purified. At this stage I call on all those who are listening with their hearts to offer themselves spontaneously, as a sacrifice to God. Your prayer shall be complete at the moment when you will offer everything, I mean everything. Let us not search for anything for ourselves, but let us offer everything to God, so that God may, through our prayers, fulfill His plan of salvation.

I am telling you – you will not be able to pray deeply until you have offered yourselves up to God.

Why do people complain, « I cannot be recollected? ». It is only natural – because we have offered up our lives to money, to earnings, to TV, because we have been offering ourselves twenty four hours a day to our earthly life and little or nothing at all to God. And given the fact that we have left such a small space for God, it is natural that we feel strained in prayer. The heart is not free, for it does not love. God is not the most important one in our lives. If you want to go forward and discover God, meditate on the Gospel every day, fast and make sacrifices as the Blessed Virgin said.

She called us to fast possibly on bread and water every Friday and possibly also every Wednesday. She called us to give up TV programmes and to devote time to God. She called on us to pray the Rosary every day.

A few days ago, a man told us he usually prays from 10 to 20 Rosaries.

I once asked through Jelena, « But when I cannot manage to finish the Rosary, is it best to meditate or to pray the Rosary? ». And I got as an answer, « *Your entire life is a Rosary* ». It means that I must pray continuously, I must be in God; I must laugh in God, I must cry in God, I must ponder in God, I must plan in God; this is continuous prayer.

Therefore I call on you – you Italians, you have many books on these events, but they are all useless if you do not get down to praying every day, be it personally, be it in the families, be it in the parishes. It will all be useless, unless you start fasting, it will all be useless unless you start confessing your sins. Our Lady invited us to a monthly confession.

And, moreover, for those who are quite advanced in their spiritual life Our Lady recommends for our prayer group, a weekly confession, « *Confess even the smallest sins, for even the smallest sin will make you suffer at the time of your meeting with Christ* ».

So there, if you want to listen to these messages, all you need to do is to put into practice all you have heard since the beginning of the Church, all you have heard from any saint – the only path leading us to a preparation, to a total opening to Christ, is prayer, conversion and fasting.

Along this path you will be able to achieve sanctity.

What I have just told you, you will find in the last message given every Thursday, when Our Lady explained how She wants to guide us all, day by day, to be more prepared and more beautiful for the Lord.

I call on you – go to confession and let your confession be the start of your conversion or the continuation of your conversion. May these events be the graces which will guide you forward in your spiritual life.

Then, one last thing I want to tell you pilgrims – when you are on your way back to Italy, remember to continue your pilgrimage towards the Immaculate Heart of Mary and towards the Sacred Heart of Jesus. Carry on living what you have been living here. Do not just come back from Medjugorje with the satisfaction that « I have achieved something and that is that! » but say to yourselves, « I have started, I must carry on ». And to end, I bless you:

By the intercession of the Blessed Virgin Mary, may God Omnipotent bless you and make you understand all the words of the Gospel and of Our Lady. May the Lord help you accomplish His plan for you.

May the Lord bless all the world's spiritual movements, may He bless all the Heads of the Church, of different religions, of different societies.

May the Lord bless all your family members, all your communities and parishes.

May He bless, most especially, all the sick and the afflicted that they may accept their difficulties and offer them to the Lord.

May the Lord bless the whole world and I bless you in the name of the Father, of the Son and of the Holy Spirit. Amen.

(Fr. Tomislav Vlašić - 26 October 1985)

Our Lady wants to clothe us with sanctity, obedience and goodness for the coming of Our Lord

Yesterday was the feast of All Saints and today of All Souls. But, before sharing some thoughts with you I will give you some news. The last apparition to Mirjana took place on 25 October, a week ago. It lasted eight minutes. During that apparition Our Lady announced to the visionary another apparition due at the end of November. She asked her to come to Medjugorje, to stay there in prayer for a few days and promised She would appear to her.

The distinctive feature of the apparition was the following: during the apparition the priest saw the visionary bow her head, she was very sad, with her eyes full of tears. After the apparition he asked her, « What happened? Why were you so sad? ». She then explained, « Our Lady showed me for the first time, as in a film, the events of Her first warning. It is very severe. That is why I am sad ». The visionary said she asked Our Lady two questions – whether these things will really take place so soon and whether God has such a hard heart. Our Lady replied, according to the visionary, that the events are imminent and that « *God does not have a hard heart, but it is you who have a hard heart – look around you, how many sins there are and you will understand* ».

I then spoke to the visionary who once again repeated, « This period is the period of grace when many graces are granted, it is the period of conversion. A second period will follow with a very painful purification for the whole of mankind and finally the meeting with Jesus Christ, after the visible sign ».

I asked the visionary how she is feeling. On the one hand she is feeling sad, on the other, however, she remarks that we must be very happy, for we know what awaits us. This life has a value, but compared with eternal life, we, here on earth are only transient.

The visionary stresses this aspect of joy and hope we must possess when looking at the future.

As you know, Our Lady sends the messages to the parish and to all the people, every Thursday. On the Thursday before last, Our Lady said She is indeed preparing us day by day; in other words, She wants to clothe us, day by day, with holiness, obedience and God's goodness, in order to make us more beautiful and more ready for the coming of the Lord.

In Her last message, the one of Thursday 31 October, Our Lady called on us all to work in the Church and asked us to work according to our capabilities. She then went on to say that we are all able to work, but we do not, because we do not feel up to it. She then said we must have courage, we must offer, each one of us, small flowers, our lives to God and that by means of these flowers, we are to make the Church and Jesus happy. She has appealed to us to contribute to the world's salvation.

I am now going to give you a thought relating to the festivity of All Saints and All Souls.

Whilst I was with people yesterday I sensed that mankind is in a crisis, that we are all in a crisis, and that can be seen also through the pilgrims who go to Medjugorje.

Such crisis is inherent in the fact that everyone talks about some trouble or other – money is short, there are many ailments around. They say that of every seven Italians, one dies of cancer.

I heard these statistics from a doctor, I do not know whether it it true or not.

Anyhow, people complain about ailments, about the lack of jobs. The world is trying through summits to stop wars. We have, however, prepared a collective suicide for mankind, for we have produced so many weapons and are capable of destroying the world. One can hear a cry of complaint everywhere and people are in a crisis.

I would like to underline three major points which ought to be three lights for us Christians.

First of all, Faith. We do not count on eternal life. For the very

174

reason, that, for us, eternal life is not a reality, but a « maybe »; we are sad, and without this faith, cannot live the feast of All Saints.

If someone were to say to you, « I want to rid you of all your problems and make you happy and blessed », what would you do? Would you like that? This is how Jesus presented Himself, yesterday. Have you considered what it means: blessed are the poor, blessed are the sad? Luckily He did not say, blessed are the rich, blessed are the powerful, blessed are those who feel well, who are in good health. But He said – blessed are you who are in a crisis. It is incredible – how is it that we Christians have not discovered this yet? How is it we do not practise it? Blessed are all of you who are in a crisis, for to you belongs the Kingdom of God.

This moment of crisis in mankind as a whole is a very favourable moment for us Christians to discover God. It is indeed a grace to discover God. Truly, I say to you – blessed are you if you have some sufferings. Not, however, are you blessed with your sorrows, but blessed are you, if you in your sorrows, discover God and eternal life.

And if really there exists a light before us for eternal life, for Heaven, for Paradise, then we become aware of the fact that ailments and difficulties are meant to be only graces for us, graces to become purified, to get closer to God through the very sufferings which come to the world. But I have seen many pilgrims put the material and earthly life in the forefront and then God, wishing Him to help us a little on this earth and after death.

With this kind of faith you cannot possibly be blessed, with this faith you will not be able to be happy here on earth and you will not enter the Kingdom of God.

All of us must place this faith in eternal life before us – our death and resurrection. We can then go towards the future with joy and blessedness, for wonderful things await us.

If only I could, in my life, do something for you, I would give you this blessedness. And you know, when you finally reach this blessedness, then neither illness nor death, nor persecution – as St. Paul says – no one will tear us apart from Christ. But not from Christ alone; nobody will separate us from joy, peace, confidence, from a happy life. There then, we must all become saints.

He who does not decide to be a saint will neither possess happiness in his heart on this earth, nor enter the Kingdom of God. It is natural for the visionary, who has seen Paradise, who has met Our Lady, to tell us to go towards the future with joy. I will tell you, however, something most important if you want to get to this blessedness. During these days, Jesus continues to lead us towards Jerusalem. Everyday during Mass we follow Luke's Gospel and slowly Jesus goes towards Jerusalem. He is determined – we can see, however, that He is wanting us also to be determined to enter this joy of His. What struck me particularly the other way, whilst I was preparing a sermon for the feast of All Saints, was the parable in St. Luke where Jesus talks about the banquet. The Lord has prepared a banquet for the guests and the servants have gone out to call the people, but they all make excuses. One was married, one had bought a field, another one... I do not know. They all were very polite, « I am sorry, I cannot come ». The Lord became angry and did not allow anyone to come in.

What impressed me is just this – they all excused themselves, they were nice about it, but no one entered the Kingdom of God.

And so the Lord gathered the people from the street to bring them to the banquet. Actually, in the face of this parable, I recognise the fact that all of us Christians are people who make excuses for themselves, « I have no time for prayer, I must go there, I must earn more ».

Look, place yourselves face to face with this parable, read the Gospel and you will see how many excuses there are within us. Excuses amount to a conviction that we do not have even one minute for God during the day. It is sometimes pretty awful, but all the kindness displayed in our excusing ourselves before the Lord is pointless. If you are invited to Milan, Parma, Rome to collect a lot of money and you never have the time to go and take it, will you ever take it? You never will. And, in the same way we behave with God. We live in a situation of practical atheism, whereby we say, « For me God is not useful, I have no time for God ».

I would really like to place this parable inside your hearts.

Follow Luke's Gospel where you will see that only the people determined to forsake everything in order to enter the Kingdom of God, will actually enter it.

Leave also your wives, husbands, also money – not to forsake them as such – but in order to put God before all else, to put Him first. As Jesus says, it is no good for me to have both eyes if I lose eternal life. I must even cut my arm off, and in this respect, we must be determined to look for the Kingdom of God. If we look for it, we shall obtain it.

Another point, another light I want to enkindle in your hearts is – love. A few days ago I spoke to a thirteen year old girl. I approached her, for I sensed she was in trouble, and as soon as I started to ask her, « How are you? », she replied, « I would say, awful ».

I started to talk a little and the girl burst into tears. Why? The girl found herself in difficulty without hope. At school she used to obtain good results, but now she only got poor ones. When she comes to church she does not behave well, she is restless. She explained her predicament.

She said, « Every year I waste my time, I cannot study, they tell me off when I go to school, they tell me off when I come home, priests tell me off when I come to church. They are all right in saying that I make mistakes, but nobody loves me ». And, indeed, I have noticed that nobody loves her. So I told her, « Let us do something about it together now, and we will start solving your problems ». We have agreed to go ahead and the little girl felt comforted.

However, in that very moment, I saw how little love there is in today's society, in the whole world, even in the Church. There are many policemen watching if someone is doing wrong or not. Unfortunately, often parents themselves have turned into policemen telling off and not understanding, for love must understand every circumstance and encourage the beneficial one. As I am talking of love and faith, I must at the same time, kindle the third light – Hope.

The girl was feeling lost, she did not know where to turn to, because she was not loved. We got down to analysing the possible ways in order to carry out this programme for her to see it through. I have told you that faith, love and hope are at the root of our salvation; we Christians must live in this root of our salvation – faith in God and in eternal life. Not just faith in something which exists after death, but faith in the sense that I must reach out for it, and today, this is most important for me.

However, only if my heart is capable of loving, will I be able to carry this light of salvation and Our Lady's messages. And I shall be able to go ahead with joy, only if I am able to bring hope.

So, if you, with all your crises, all your complaints, all your ailments, offer your lives and set out on your path with these lights of faith, love and hope, you will be happy from the very start.

If you want to experience this, offer your lives to God.

If you receive a hundred million Lire it will never make you happy, but when you share some of your own with your neighbour, when you offer your lives – together with all your ailments – to God, then you will finally attain blessedness, happiness.

Last Thursday, Our Lady, in Her message to the prayer group, amongst other things, said, « *God loves you much, He loves you a hundred times more than your parents* », and Our Lady wanted them to offer and open their hearts to this love.

I would just like to underline these words once again – God loves us a thousand times more than our parents. So, we too, let us open our hearts at this very moment when this love on God's part is being manifested also through the Blessed Virgin who is teaching us how to reach the house of the Father.

In a message, Our Lady said, « *If you want to be stronger than evil and grow in goodness, then make yourselves an active conscience* »; in other words, pray a lot, after you have prayed, read a passage of the Gospel, take the Word of the Gospel, plant it in your hearts and cultivate it during the day. In my opinion, this is the path of resurrection. Many confessions become almost futile because those concerned are exactly the same the following day, carrying on behaving like before. Many pilgrimages have failed and people have been worshiping in several sanctuaries and on coming home, simply say, « I have done it », and that is that. If you want to grow in strength, you must pray every day, you must seek the Word of the Lord which heals the soul, which brings forward and increases grace, which makes us stronger, which makes us grow in faith, love and hope. You will then become stronger and stronger, more and more spiritually enlightened. It is exactly this I wanted to emphasise – on going back to Italy from Medjugorje, I would ask you to continue your pilgrimage towards God, towards the Word of God.

O Lord Jesus Christ, I beseech you, by the intercession of the Blessed Virgin Mary, look upon all these pilgrims, open their hearts to a true faith, to a true love and true hope.

Lord Jesus Christ, you want to save everyone, you seek all men, and are happy with Your Mother, because you see the pilgrims here and their intentions. I beg you, help them so that they may, each one of them, open their hearts.

Jesus, help them so that they may live Your blessedness in the crisis in which they live. I beg You to bless all the sick, all the suffering, all people suffering of any kind of problem whatsoever, so that they may all feel the blessedness.

Jesus Christ, I beg You for grace, that each pilgrim may answer Your call without excuses and live for eternal life. I beg You for decision, so that each of them may be determined to belong totally to You, to leave all that is hindering them from reaching You.

Please, O Lord Jesus Christ, open their hearts to accept the gifts You and Your Mother are giving to everyone here present and to the whole of mankind. Send Your Spirit, so that these people may understand Your answer in their hearts. Send Your Spirit to bless their families, their parishes, their communities, their hospitals. Send Your Spirit to bless their country and the whole world.

And I bless you in the name of the Father, of the Son and of the Holy Spirit. Amen.

I say good-bye to you. Best wishes, and have a good journey.

(Fr. Tomislav Vlašić - 2 November 1985)

To believe means to commit oneself to God

Welcome.

It is fifty-four months now since the beginning of the apparitions, this is a very long story, a world event.

We have allowed all possible experiments to be carried out so as to make sure, to find out what is happening and one can now say that medicine, psychology, pathology have no more to say. What is now left is theology, pastoral spirituality, mysticism to explore, to carry on researching all that is happening here.

What does Our Lady want in so many months of apparitions? Peace. Our Lady has entrusted peace in our hands, we are responsible for it. She is thus showing a great trust in us, by asking us to help Her in bringing peace to this world.

Our Lady, as a Mother, is calling on us to help Her to bring peace to this world – how can we do it? She said, quite simply, « *Pray and fast* ».

To recite the Creed every day means to commit oneself to God – I give you my life today, at every moment, in every difficulty, in my suffering, in my work, in my study; I know who I belong to. This is the Creed. Our Lady wants us to pray every day, so that each day may be an impulse, a path towards the Lord.

Our Lady, as a Mother, wants to be with us and She can only be with us if we devote time to Her, by meditating on Her life and coming closer to Her life with our lives.

Recently I was talking to a Bishop in Ireland. He told me, « I have heard of Medjugorje, of the messages, but one thing is bothering me somewhat, these daily apparitions, why? ».

I replied, « Our Lady knows the answer. I can only speak for myself. Our Lady is a Mother and, as a Mother, wants to be in every family every day, not just on Sundays when one goes to Mass. She wants to be there every day and She can, provided we take time for the Rosary ».

All this must be a means for us to change our life and every day deepen our faith, love, peace and reconciliation.

I am sure that each one of you who has started to pray has met some sort of difficulty in prayer – he is distracted and so on. But it does not matter. Do not be afraid when you are faced with these difficulties, just go on. As far as fasting is concerned, Our Lady said, ideally twice a week on bread and water.

Fasting certainly helps prayer. One can pray better when one is fasting and one can fast better when praying.

Fasting also helps faith – one can hear the Word of the Lord better. To fast means to come out of ourselves, from the broken home of our hearts in order to hear the Lord. Fasting purifies us and faith also comes from listening; in this way, we are better prepared to listen to the Word, which inside a heart which is free from materialism and selfishness, can more readily become active, and change our lives.

Fasting also helps love, for, by fasting, one becomes a bit more open, one is more sensitive to the other, to our neighbour, one can more easily see that we have plenty, that we really must think more of others. When you fast, the principle to follow in order to know whether you are fasting well or not, is to feel whether prayer is growing deeper, whether you are praying more easily, whether you are feeling more sorrow when you have done something to offend someone else. This means that we are becoming more sensitive and this is the only way to reach peace.

The Thursday messages help us to deepen the messages of peace, conversion, faith and prayer.

Three weeks ago Our Lady asked us once again, to be thankful, to learn how to be thankful, even for the smallest of things. This is another word for peace. When do I say, thank you? When should I say, thank you? Who can say thank you? The one who sees the other, who recognises the other, who is humble. One can read in the Magnificat how Our Lady was thankful. Not to say thank you, not to be grateful, not to have any gratitude in one's heart – this is the greatest atheism.

Think of the story of Adam and Eve – they received everything from the Lord, but in one moment, they forgot, they became blind to what the Lord had given them; they wanted to sin, they felt they had to sin in the hope of receiving even more. They became blind. This is the deepest form of atheism. Who can give everything to a selfish person? When will a selfish person ever say thank you? If he were to be given the whole world, it would not be enough. When can a proud person say thank you? Even if you do everything for him, it will not be enough. He who is humble sees the others, he sees the smallest of things, he starts thanking. If one does that, then peace comes to families, peace comes to the world. I am telling you this in order to be able to be thankful – the way Our Lady is asking – one must pray, one must confess, one must fast.

Therefore, it is necessary to see in order to thank.

When you receive these Thursday messages, always try and deepen them, try and find a connection with the other messages, because there is always a reason why Our Lady gives the messages.

You know that recently She said She wants to guide us, She wants us to be full of peace, joy, conversion, like a new dress.

This is yet another word for peace, to have a new dress of goodness, of love.

When Our Lady says, a new dress of love, of peace, we must think of those clothes which have been torn by sin. It is always a sin which breaks a person, a community, a Church. Sin always breaks, and the new dress is love, peace.

In Her last message, She invited us all to be active in the Church, to bring one's own flowers to the church, to Jesus, and added that everyone should be happy. When Our Lady says we must be active, this means we are capable of being so. Our Lady knows who She is talking to, which means there is no one, even if sick, who can say, « What can I do? ».

Think of St. Paul's comparison between the body and the Church – the eye cannot say to the head, « I do not need you », nor can the head say to the leg, « I do not need you ». We all have many charisms, we have received many graces and can serve the Church and Jesus.

And when I look at myself positively, when I acknowledge the fact that I have received a lot, I also feel responsible for going ahead. Our Lady wants this.

The whole logic of these apparitions can be said in the one word Our Lady told Marija, I believe two months ago.

During one of the apparitions Marija asked, « Blessed Virgin, do you have something specific for me? ». The answer was, « *Yes, I have. I give you my love, so that you may give it to others* ». This is the logic, « I give you my love, my peace, reconciliation, everything, all the graces, so that you may give them to others ». If in these days, in these times we are without peace, without love, without reconciliation, this means we have not opened our hands.

(Fr. Slavko Barbarić - 2 November 1985)

«I am your Mother, I love you and wish to urge you continuously to prayer»

Queen of Peace, pray for us.

I greet you all and want to explain a little what the present position is like here with the visionaries and tell you something about the spirituality of the messages.

The visionaries who still have apparitions from Our Lady every night are now four: Vicka, Marija, Jakov and Ivan.

Our Lady has been telling Vicka the future of the world since 17 April of this year. Nothing special about her health. She has headaches.

Sometimes they say she has a cancer, a tumour, but it is not so. Nobody knows. It seems to me it is something mystical.

Anyway, what the doctors have told her is, «You need rest». They are perhaps the symptoms of fatigue. You can imagine – in ten days' time it will have been 54 months since it all started. It is an extremely long story as regards the apparitions. In these days she is in Zagreb. A new doctor of the Commission has asked for Vicka to go to Zagreb for a check up.

Marija Pavlović has apparitions like Vicka. And through Marija Our Lady has been giving messages every Thursday since 1 March 1984.

If anyone wants the messages, they can read them on the notice board of the church. And if anyone wants all the messages in addition to a few comments of Fr. Tomislav and my own, they can write to the Association of Friends of Medjugorje of Milan. [1] A second volume has now also been published. [2]

---

[1] The book is: « Open your hearts to Mary Queen of Peace ».
[2] The book is: « Abandon Yourselves Totally to Me ».

184

Today they have given me a copy of the first book – it is the one hundred thousandth copy – a major work, surely, for Our Lady and us all.

There are also some people who, week by week, pass on the messages to others, you can take their phone numbers at the entrance to the church.

Our Lady is telling Jakov the world's future and through Ivan She is leading a prayer group.

Ivanka has not had any apparitions since the 7 May of this year. Our Lady has promised her an apparition for the anniversary of the apparitions; 25 June 1986 should be the first apparition since the end of the daily ones.

To Mirjana Our Lady has not been appearing since Christmas 1982; She has, however, been appearing on her birthday. Mirjana is now having internal conversations. During these conversations Our Lady is talking a lot about the secrets and invites us to prayer, Mirjana said, particularly for the unbeliever.

Mirjana has chosen the priest to whom she will confide the secrets; it is Fr. Pero of our community.

Mirjana received her last conversations in Medjugorje – she came from Serajevo.

Mirjana said she saw the first secret as if in a film and said, « My God, does this really have to happen? ». Our Lady is supposed to have answered that it is not God but sin that does it.

Owing to this piece of news I feel that many have been overcome with fear, with anguish. And many very much wonder – why pray if these things are to happen, why fast, why work?

I wish to tell you how I have interpreted these apocalyptic messages. In the New Testament we have a Book bearing the name of Apocalypse. In this book you can read of many dreadful things St. John saw in his visions and described, many disasters... But you see, all this cannot be explained just in terms of physical catastrophe; this must always be interpreted in terms of conversion.

The first stage of these messages, despite the fact that they seem terrible, is the call to conversion. In other words – they help our faith. Our faith must always have this quality of waiting.

To wait, also for this reason there is fasting.

For two days a week I leave the earthly values behind, I really forsake them and wait for my Lord.

And so, if our faith does not have this dimension, it is not Christian faith in the full sense of the word.

Sometimes I say that many, with their faith, remain trapped in this world – they eat and drink, with money they intend to organise their lives, the lives of their families, but do not possess this very quality that makes you say – I must be ready every day for the Lord.

You probably know what St. Augustine did so many times. He used to repeat, « Conversion, not today but tomorrow », but for all of us the contrary applies, « Conversion is truly for to-day ». Think of Jesus' parable about the foolish and wise virgins – five of them waited for the bridegroom and went in with him, whilst the foolish ones did not wait for him. They had lost the quality of faith. And they could not wait.

In the New Testament, mostly in the Apocalypse, there is a word which the Church has been repeating many times, Maranatha! In other words, come Lord Jesus!

The visionaries have lived this quality of faith which opens the world of the hereafter and which awaits with hope.

There is no room for anguish, for fear. Even when hearing of these things, if we have fear, it shows that we have no faith or our faith is very weak.

Last night I spoke to the three visionaries, Marija, Ivan and Jakov also about this vision of Mirjana's and asked, « Are you afraid? ». They replied, « No, we are not ». Mark my words, this is a sign of faith, to always have confidence.

And there is something else. In his letter to the Thessalonians, St. Paul writes about someone who, having heard that Jesus was about to come, did not want to work anymore. St. Paul said, « Very well, if he does not wish to work, do not let him eat either... ».

I repeat, all these messages will have no meaning for us if we respond with fear. We must respond with confidence, with love and say, « Everything is in God's hands and today I need to carry out all my duties with love and hope ».

This I have understood and this I tell everyone – the apparitions never bear a new revelation; they are always an impulse to pray, to fast, to love, to be reconciled, to make peace.

And so not even these secret messages can bring anything new. They merely encourage our faith to become once more alive and that we do not go to sleep.

I now want to talk to you about the latest messages; yesterday we received a very beautiful message, full of Motherly feeling, of Motherly love – « *Dear children. I, your Mother who loves you, want to urge you to pray without ceasing. I am, dear children, tireless and I call you even when you are far away from my heart. I feel sorrow for anyone who is getting lost. But I am your Mother and I forgive easily and I am happy for every child who comes back to Me. Thank you for responding to my call* ».

She twice repeated, « *I am your Mother* » and tells us She will never be tired. She wants to save us, She wants to urge us on and, naturally, also talks about Her sorrow. Someone who loves may also have sorrow. Our Lady is not indifferent to someone lost in sin, in conflict, in war, in drugs, in alcohol... so She feels the sorrow and says once again, « *I am your Mother and I easily forgive, I am glad, happy, joyful, full of joy for anyone who comes back, who returns* ». This is a real chance for us – there we have a Mother's heart who loves us, who wants to save us.

If I may add a word to this message, that is – you and I having heard this message must pray every day for all those who are in sin, who are in enmities, who hate, who are not reconciled, that they may receive the grace of reconciliation.

Let us help Our Lady to save us.

In Her last message She has asked for love towards our neighbour. Above all She said, « *Love those who cause you evil* ».

The love of one's enemy, as Jesus asked. It is at this very point that Christian love starts.

If we do not want to forgive, we cannot say we love in Jesus'
sense. And peace begins with forgiveness. If we do not love those
who cause us evil, Jesus will ask us, as He already has – what is
special in your loving those who love you?

Another phrase of this message was, « *love in order to be able to
value your hearts' intentions* ». So you see, She is here giving a rule
whereby one can get to know a man's heart. And this is true.
Without love we cannot see the other person; without love we start
judging, without love we slander, without love we hate, without
love we come to blows with others; but when there is love we
acquire a new gauge, a new measure for man.

Even someone who hates, who causes us evil, there is still a man
behind this provocation, behind this hate, behind this conflict in
need of peace and of being loved. And many people who do evil
have already been judged by us. They were searching for love,
searching for peace. There was no one around who could give it to
them and the whole thing has turned into evil, into sin.

The third issue of the same message is this, « *Love and pray so
that even impossible things become possible* ». So you see, in this
love, this prayer to which Our Lady is inviting us we can find very
strong means which can make even the impossible, possible.

This is a chance for us, a great opportunity, but also a duty not
to dismiss anything as impossible in our lives.

In one of the messages She asked for our good works. She said,
« *I want you all to do good works* ». She wants us, with our little
flowers, to help the Church and Jesus so that all of us may be happy.

When Our Lady says, « *Activity for us all* », this means that no
one of us can say, « I cannot do anything ».

And the prime activity is prayer. It is with prayer that we can make
possible even the impossible.

Other good works are: to visit the sick, to think of the poor, to
help, to console, to think of others...

If we do so, perhaps we shall be surprised when Jesus will say,
« Come blessed ones into my Kingdom, for you have visited me,
you have fed me... ». We might ask, « How can this be? I visited
someone else, I have visited a sick man, I helped a poor man... ».

Jesus will say, « Yes, you have. But all you have done for that person, you have done it for me ». Again, I tell you – this is the gate to Christian love; to be active and never allow oneself to become weary.

Tiredness can be overcome, Our Lady says, in prayer.

In another message Our Lady asked for, among other things, our consecration to the Cross, « *Pray before the Cross. From the Cross great graces come. Be consecrated to the Cross. Promise not to offend Jesus in the Cross* ».

This is a crucial point – to be consecrated to the Cross means to feel the Cross. And the Cross is an expression on love, on sacrifice. on eternal life. It is from the Cross that it is said, « Here is your Mother, here is your son ».

And how do we behave before the Cross? Perhaps we do not forgive, perhaps we get into conflict, perhaps we swear. If we do so, the Cross becomes dumb, it does not speak to us anymore.

Instead, for us to be consecrated means to hear the Cross, to allow it to speak. And for Italians, Slavs and Hungarian people this message is most important.

Some of you may not know that these people have the worst swear words in the world.

As I was exorcising an Italian pilgrim, I heard, during prayer, all your swear words. All the time while I was saying in my prayer of exorcism – Jesus, the Cross, Our Lady, the Church, God, there followed swear words...

If one reacts in this manner to prayer, this is also a sign of obsession. I do not know how one excuses oneself in your country; here with us one says, « I am angry, I am nervous, my work is not going as I had wanted... I swear, but I do not mean to in my heart... ».

I do believe one does not mean it in one's heart, but I do not know whether Our Lady accepts these excuses.

Let us promise not to offend Jesus and the Cross with our swearing anymore. But let us do more than that – we are not Christians not to offend, we are Christians to act positively. Every swear word I may perhaps hear in future in the family, on the bus, on the train, in the street, at work, will be an impulse for me to pray, to praise, to bless... to pray for him who is swearing – so do not judge, but pray.

Therefore, this evening, before the blessing, at the end of the prayer for the sick, when I say to you, « Consecrate yourselves to the Cross », say a word to Jesus in your hearts, your own word. And I will pray to Our Lady that She may become a reality for all of us, that from the Cross great graces may come to us.

(Fr. Slavko Barbarić - 15 November 1985)

All those who listen to Our Lady's messages belong to her parish

Our Lady is calling us to conversion and, if She is asking for our hand, if She has been telling us so many times in Her messages, «*I want to guide you*», She does not want to guide us to a catastrophe, but She wants to save us. And in this respect it is wrong to respond with no reaction on our part – not to work, not to pray because everything is anyway predetermined.

No, if we give our hand to Our Lady, She is going to lead not just us personally, but the whole world on to the right path, the path to peace. We know catastrophes are possible because they come from nature or from man, who can and does destroy.

For this reason Our Lady invites us to prayer.

And something more – our faith must have an apocalyptic quality, that is the quality of waiting for the Lord. Jesus told many parables where He stressed this very quality – not to sleep, but to be awake. Our faith must be alive in the sense of a new tone, a new standard in our lives.

How many times Jesus said, « We live in this world, but are not of this world ». And we Christians have lost this quality and behave in our families, in our conflicts, as if we did not believe. Many live unreconciled, many do not forgive, many neglect the sick, the poor... and yet claim to be Christians. This quality of live, active faith must come back into our life, it must stir it and give it once more new vigour.

At present Marija is at a spiritual retreat for young people who want to live this spirituality, to live the messages.

Our Lady gives the messages through Marija every Thursday – these you already know.

Our Lady is telling Jakov the world's future. He goes to school in the afternoon and receives the apparitions after Mass.

Through Ivan, Our Lady leads a prayer group and guides them in prayer. Yesterday, Ivan gave me a programme for the spiritual exercises which Our Lady is asking of this group.

I would like to talk to you about this. And it is this that we must learn by heart and remember rather than that which is curious. Ivan told me of the various apparitions and how Our Lady wants this group to do these spiritual exercises.

You already know that this group meets twice to pray on the mountain – on Mondays and on Fridays. During prayer, Our Lady appears to Ivan, Marija and Vicka if they are on the mountain. Ivan is always present and Marija nearly always.

Our Lady said that next week there will be no apparitions with the group – each one will have to do these exercises individually. The most important means are the Bible and the Rosary. Our Lady has asked them to pray three times a day, to go into silence as much as possible and also to sing and read the Bible. In this way they will receive peace, they will be able to live better, and better understand the messages.

During these days of spiritual retreat She has asked them not to watch television, not to listen to the radio, to retire, but always remaining within the manner of their normal lives. They should retire and pray as much as possible. She also asked these young people not to smoke, not to go to the coffee bar, not to talk too much about other things, but to make « tac »; does one say that with you as well? That is to say, not to talk about trivial things. They then should attend Mass every evening; they should live Mass the way Our Lady asked of all of us in a message – one should prepare oneself, so that Mass may indeed become a live experience of God.

Our Lady is asking them to pay attention, to prepare themselves, to celebrate Mass and to thank Our Lord after Mass. They will then be able to understand the messages, to live them, to put them into practice in their daily lives.

This seems to me very important and we should experience all this, each one in our own individual way.

Our Lady has promised this group, but surely each one of us as well, both help and special graces. When you are back home, let everyone act according to their own possibilities. Our Lady asked to pray still more on days of fasting. Our Lady is asking this group for individual prayer and group-prayer, whereby the members pray, sing and sometimes pray in twos.

If the group is made up of fifteen members, for example, let them pray the Rosary in twos. Our Lady explained why – it is very important to get to know one another in a group where people pray together. If we always pray together within a group there is the risk of becoming rather impersonal with relation to each other. And so She has asked for one Rosary to be said on one's own, one in the group and the third part in twos. Sometimes they have prayed two parts together and, as for the third, She has said, « *Go to your homes and before the Cross, pray the third part on your own* ».

So, by changing method or by combining several prayer methods together, She wants to help these young people to grow in prayer. There are other points, but I have told you what is essential.

The aim is this – to better understand the messages.

Our Lady is asking of us all the Creed and seven Our Fathers every day, the whole Rosary, the reading of the Bible; fasting twice a week and confession once a month. Mass should be attended as often as possible and, as I have already told you, with active participation – one should prepare oneself before Mass and give thanks after Mass. In this way you will also understand the liturgy of this evening – we start one hour beforehand with the Rosary; Our Lady comes before Mass, She blesses us, She leads us – so to speak – to Mass, to Jesus.

This is Her first task – to lead us to Jesus. He is the source of peace, reconciliation and love.

And afterwards, we also give thanks.

This is the way we have understood it and try to live these messages in our parish, in our community and with the pilgrims who come here.

This is very important – by following this experience one day it may even be possible for other people to also pray this way in their own parishes.

I know of many people forming prayer groups; in their parishes they have a day of prayer as in Medjugorje.

This is the true and sound response.

So if we pray, we are always united.

And when Our Lady says, « *I cherish this parish* », do not just think of the parish of Medjugorje. All those who listen to Our Lady's messages belong to Her parish, and conversely, if someone here in this parish is not listening, I very much doubt whether he belongs actively to it.

Our Lady is asking for active prayer also in families. I ask you – who is there in your families, who is active in prayer? Who organises it? Who chooses a passage of the Gospel? Who says, « Enough now with T.V., with the radio, with music, with the telephone. Now let us pray »?

Who lights a candle in a little corner and in it places a Cross and the Bible, saying, « Let us pray here? ».

As it is natural to say that a mother prepares breakfast, lunch, supper; that someone is in charge of the car, of the household chores, and so it may seem a bit strange to ask who is in charge of prayer in the family.

Let us all become in some degree responsible and we shall more easily find time for prayer. The first prayer group must be in the family. When Our Lady is asking for activity from us, one must understand by that as being active in the family. I know of families where the father says who is supposed to prepare prayers on Mondays, on Tuesday, on Wednesdays... then in this way one learns how to pray.

Our Lady is also asking for fasting; it is quite clear – as one must pray, so must one fast. And when we have fasted and prayed, all other things will be given to us. All this is brought about thanks to the peace in our hearts, in our families and in the entire world.

Our Lady has made us responsible for peace and there is a lot we can do. All we receive we must in turn give to others in order to receive more ourselves. If we Christians, in this time of special grace, are left without peace, without love, if we remain in our conflicts, it is a sign of our not having opened our hands, of not having opened our hearts.

Our Lady told us in a message, « *I am at the door and knock at the door of many hearts, but many do not open. Pray with me* ». And now something concerning the messages.

Our Lady said, « *Dear children, I am your Mother* » and repeated it twice.

Every message is full of motherly feeling. When She says, « *Dear children* » and when She thanks you « *for responding to...* », even though She knows we have not all responded, not all responded well. Like a Mother, She sees even the smallest things and says thanks. Here the Motherhood of Our Lady shows itself as clear as the sun; like a Mother She loves us, like a Mother – I say – She does not leave us alone until we have found peace, until we have found love. She wants to urge us to prayer all the time because prayer is the way to go forward, and says: « *I am never tired, I shall always invite you* ». She does not accept our excuses when we say, « I have no time, I have no... ».

« *I call you, even when you are far away* », like a mother who does not give up her son, even when he goes away, when he does not write, when he does not telephone. She does not give up, she prays and is happy, she is full of joy if he returns.

Our Lady like our mother feels great sorrow for anyone who is getting lost. Again, She says, « *I am your Mother, I easily forgive and I am full of joy for each one of you who returns* ». I call on you – tonight as well, let us pray not just for all of us to become faithful, but for us to help Our Lady try and save all those who are getting lost.

In Her other messages, She has invited us to be consecrated to the Cross, to love our neighbour, to forgive, to learn once again to say thank you for the smallest things, so that we may also be thankful for the greater things.

I have told you She is asking for good works in the Church, that is, asking for our faith to become alive.

Well, I thank you. You may know of many other things, you might have known of these as well, nevertheless one always gets a fresh impulse for prayer, fasting, faith, reconciliation and conversion from them.

(Fr. Slavko Barbarić - 16 November 1985)

« You have forgotten you are in my hand »

I greet you all, welcome.

First of all I want to give you some news on Medjugorje; I am then going to share with you a few thoughts I feel within me.

Our Lady is continuing, through the visionaries who see Her daily, to invite the world to conversion, prayer, fasting, peace.

Through Vicka She is telling us of certain events of the future of the Church and the world; for the last month She has started to tell also Jakov some of the events.

Usually, every Thursday night, through Marija, She has been giving messages to the Parish and people in general.

Through Ivan, She is leading a prayer group. Every day during the apparitions, Ivan and Marija commend the sick.

Now some news regarding Jakov – he came round to the Parish office and said, « I wish to become a friar and I want to go into a seminary straightaway ». We asked, « But why? For what reason? ». He replied, « I just want to become a Friar and that is it ». He immediately went up to the Father Provincial to ask for permission, but the Father Provincial replied, « Wait a little to see how you can be fitted into the school as the course has already started ». However, he did not seem upset by this, but on the contrary, he decided to take up Latin with Fr. Slavko immediately, and said, « If I cannot go to the seminary soon, then I will finish the current school year and carry on with the seminary next year, so that I can become a Friar ».

This attitude of Jakov is typical of the visionaries, for they display a growth, a maturity in full response to Our Lady's and God's plan.

Then there are particular moments for Ivanka who – as you already know – has not seen Our Lady since 7 May; Ivanka simply feels a great desire to pray and be with Our Lady, with her heart. The main feature of news is connected with Mirjana, the girl who has received the task of warning the world of the first three secrets, three admonishments to mankind.

The visionary tells of being aware of the weight of sin in the world and accepts this reality on the level of faith as something normal; she stresses the fact that this is a period of grace for mankind, that is, when many graces are granted and when Heaven is calling the world to salvation; the second period being one of harsh purification of mankind and the third one, the one of God's manifestation. When we look and listen to all these messages, we notice a line of invitation, of continuous call on people to prayer, just as Our Lady said in Her last message, « *I am tireless in calling you to prayer* ». Our Lady is sad when any of Her children get lost, whereas She is happy to call them to come back to Her once again. Indeed, all the Thursday messages are a continuous call for everyone to draw closer to God.

I would now like to consider deeply with you the following – are you all Christians? Do you remember last Sunday's Gospel?

Do you know why I am asking you this question? Because many Christians cannot remember it anymore. This year I have had a particular experience of my own – during the week I feel like a little boy who is attending a class, who must finish his lessons. If, by chance, I do not manage to finish what Our Lord has set for me to do for the week, I have failed, I feel I have failed. I am telling you all this because I feel a rhythm in the liturgy; every Sunday, with its message, is a step forward to progress and I have discovered that I have not been practising it, I have not been living it every day step by step. And I see how so many Christians do not follow it, do not know it.

Last Sunday we were presented with that widow who gave some coppers, but she gave more than everyone else, for she gave all she had. In the first reading there was that widow who gave the last handful of flour, her very last one, to the prophet Elijah, but the container did not become empty, for she gave everything. I set about following this message in order to empty myself, but not just to empty myself in order to give something of my own, but also to leave self behind.

And by virtue of this rhythm I have, indeed, come to ponder on today's Gospel and on tomorrow's Gospel and readings.

Do you know what today's and tomorrow's message is for us? The message is this – tomorrow we shall hear words of future events, even disastrous ones. Although the Prophet Daniel is talking of the last happenings, and Jesus is talking of terrible things that will occur on earth, there is in all this, nevertheless, a message for us – of peace, confidence, joy, a very deep life. I am talking to you today because I would like you all to be ready to accept this message. Look, in tomorrow's psalm is written: « The Lord is my inheritance and my chalice; you have my fate in your hands ».

God has taken you by the hand, he is holding you in His hand. It would suffice to meditate on this, to feel oneself in God's hand; it is wonderful. You cannot understand the messages of the visionaries, when they are talking of the world's future, even of harsh things, unless you are able to understand that you are in God's hand.

If you do not grasp this you will be people who are waiting for the future full of fear. Instead, you are in God's hand.

You will only be able to achieve this attitude and appreciate this liturgy of tomorrow by which you will experience that you are in God's hand with all your problems, through today's Gospel.

Jesus invites us to pray continuously, not to leave God alone – so to speak – to really bother Him with our prayer, and He will answer it. And the Gospel ends with, « But when the Son of God comes, will He still find faith on earth? ». I ask myself and you this question – what does this mean?

Our Lord is calling us to continuous prayer – many pilgrims come and pray, pray, pray, and Our Lord says, « Shall I find faith when I come? ».

To my mind it is very important to know this – whether we really are persistent in prayer or not. When it is a question of persisting in prayer, it is not just a matter of time – I pray all day long – but also a matter of quality of prayer, it means reaching God's full depth, succeeding in understanding God's will.

Yesterday, I read a message from a mystic who says she has received this message herself, « Jesus tells me, "There are two types of prayer; one where you talk and I listen and the other, where you listen and I talk". So the mystic asked, "Which of these prayers do you like most?" He answered, "The second one, where I talk and you listen" ». I must say, there are very few people able to listen to God when He is talking. I will give you an example: while I was with a small group which Our Lady chose, we prayed for an hour and finally together with the visionary, we listened to the message Jesus had given through her, « *You have forgotten you are in my hand* ». Suddenly I saw how the entire process of our prayer – of over an hour – had been almost a complaint: give us, give us, give us; whereas we have everything. We do, in fact, have everything, but as we had not listened to Our Lord with our hearts, we kept asking Him to give us this, to give us that. But He does act for us, for He holds us in His hand; indeed, He works for us far more than we pray to Him; He is with us, He takes care of us.

However, we can experience Our Lord's care for us only if we have emptied ourselves totally, as that widow did, and when we are completely open. And I must tell you something difficult, very difficult indeed, and in this respect you will have to make an examination of conscience – you must offer your sins, your worries to the Lord. But you all wish to give your worries away and keep them for yourselves at the same time. We have not yet learned to be abandoned, to offer our worries to the Lord. So I have understood why Jesus said, « When I come on earth, will I find faith? ». We often, in fact, pray as long as it is to our benefit and as far as what we consider logical but when trials and difficulties approach, we withdraw.

We cannot pray in depth if we are not capable of abandoning ourselves to Our Lord in our trials, accepting from God's hand the very things which are unfavourable to our lives, as something more positive.

When it comes to illness, when it comes to slander, when it comes to injustice, when it comes to lack of money, when it comes to trouble of any kind in your lives, are you capable, at that moment, of being joyful, of saying « This is the right opportunity for me to discover God in depth, for me to make progress ». Until we adopt this attitude, our prayer will not be persistent; in fact, we are not praying, but are wanting something for ourselves; we are not seeking God to the utmost. This is lack of faith, because faith is listening fully to Jesus Christ and God. Faith is not, « I believe in God ». In that case, the whole of mankind believes in God. So much so, that I do believe that, in theory, atheists do not exist, for they could not find sufficient reasons for which to reject God; but we all have faith, we are all faithful to a certain degree, but not the kind of faith Our Lord wants, faith as total listening to the Lord. So you see, a total listening, a listening which is carried out to the end, means persistence in prayer and faith, the kind of faith the Lord is looking for at this moment.

If you want to verify whether your faith is true, then examine yourselves in the moments of trial. I say to you – the most beautiful periods with Our Lord are the periods of trials. If you are not prepared to go through your trials with Our Lord, to accept His explanation in your difficulties, then you cannot take your exams, you have failed.

We are getting close to the festivity, and which festivity are we in the Novena of...? Of Christ the King. Unfortunately there are very few people indeed who prepare themselves for this festivity with a novena, but it is most important, it really means to qualify for the specialisation, not just for the degree course, but to open ourselves so that Jesus may reign in our hearts.

If you want to go forward you are left only with the path Our Lady has pointed out to you – pray, more and more, pray with your heart. Today's Gospel, indeed the last phrase, shows you the way – to pray, but to pray in order to persist in prayer, in trials, for you all know that the most wicked people in the street would accept God if only He were to be conformed to their wishes. But, if we who are in the Church, who pray, then go and behave in the same manner, what difference is there between us and them? A very narrow one. This is why we are not reaching these fruits of peace and joy and are not able to look at the future with peace and joy, even though our future may be difficult.

I wish for each one of us to acquire this deep attitude of abandonment to God, in order to live tomorrow's message. Notice, something wonderful will be said tomorrow, when St. Paul talks of the High Priest Jesus, who does not need to offer thousands of sacrifices – He has offered everything for us, once and for all.

I wish that all of us may be able to appreciate this truth – God has offered everything for us. To finish our liturgical exam of the year, indeed, means to find ourselves saved in Jesus, full of joy. It means to wait with joy for our own death, to wait with joy for our meeting with the Lord, to wait for Heaven, to wait for our eternal life, and to go ahead with joy.

If you have this deep Christian attitude, then you will see, all of you who have come to Medjugorje burdened with worries, you will be relieved of your worries, of your troubles.

As far as the future is concerned, many people ask about it, about the secrets, about the messages. Tomorrow you will get a wonderful explanation.

In Mark's Gospel, Chapter 13, Jesus says, « From the figtree learn this lesson – as soon as its branch becomes tender and puts forth its leaves, you know that summer is near. So also, when you see these things happen, you will know that He is at the door ». And the second passage, « Truly, truly, I say to you, this generation shall not pass, before all these things will have happened. Heaven and earth will pass away, but my words will not pass away. As for the day and hour, nobody knows them, not even the Angels in Heaven, nor the Son, but only the Father ». Have you understood? God hidden and God revealed. God is hiding the future; not even the Son knows the dates, but God is talking to our hearts and we are able to understand this moment.

The visionaries have been given certain things, certain secrets, not – as many believe – a mathematical prevision of the future. These things they have been given so that we, by pondering within our hearts, may understand the present moment of the world. If our minds do not know the future dates in a rational sense, our hearts are able to understand the path to take. What should we do? You well know what we must do. We must take the steps of the prodigal son. We must draw near to the Father's house and when we are close to it, then we shall see and will be in His arms. Unfortunately, many are far away from the Father in their own sins and say, « We will see whether the apparitions are true or not ». Many expect the Father to come into the solitude of the Prodigal Son and manifest Himself there, but this could never happen. God is waiting, God is calling, and it is up to us to take the path. In the same way a son, a boy who has failed at school must undertake to study in order to take his exams and hopefully pass; similarly, mankind must grasp in its heart the path it must take in order to reach the Father. But surely, we know the path, we must try, however, not to philosophize too much. Peace – mankind will not be saved without peace, we all know it, both atheists and believers. We must commit ourselves to God.

We must change, change our lifestyle; atheists say so, believers also say so. They both say – mankind must be changed. Some make revolutions with weapons, others make a spiritual revolution, but both agree – mankind must be changed; justice, love and equality must come to the world.

If we are believers, then we know what prayer and fasting mean for us – they are the most suitable means to promote a change in the world, as a positive change, without offending or hurting anybody.

One must promote peace, promote love, promote human dignity by Jesus Christ's means; not a revolution with the sword, but a revolution by means of love, by means of peace.

There, I wanted to share this with you.

(Fr. Tomislav Vlašić - 16 November 1985)

« Prepare yourselves for Christmas with prayer, penance and works of love »

When Mirjana announced the content of the last before one locution, many telephoned to ask, « Has She already told you when, how...? ». And many were also frightened. I also heard some people saying, « If something is bound to happen, if we cannot stop it, then why work, why pray, why fast? ». All reactions like these are false.

These messages are apocalyptic, and in order to understand them, one needs perhaps to read once again the Apocalypse of St. John or Jesus' address in the Gospel admonishing his listeners.

During these last two Sundays you have been hearing of signs of the stars and many other things – when will this happen? Jesus said, « Soon ». But this « soon » is not to be gauged in our days or months.

These apocalyptic messages have a purpose – our faith must be awake and not asleep.

Remember some of Jesus' parables, when He talked about the ten virgins, five of who were wise and five foolish – what did the foolishness of the foolish ones consist of? They thought, « The bridegroom will not come so early », they were not ready and could not go to dinner with the bridegroom.

Our faith must always have this dimension.

Think of the other parable of Jesus, in which is said, « ... my soul rejoice now for you have enough to eat and drink », and the Lord says, « Fool, what will you do if this night your soul is required of you? And to whom will you leave all you have gathered? ».

One element of faith is the element of waiting, of keeping vigilant. The apocalptic messages require us to be awake, not to sleep as regards our faith, our peace with God, with others, and as regards our conversion... there is no need to be afraid, there is no need to say, « This soon? Then there is no need to work or pray anymore... ».

A reaction of this kind is false.

These messages are to enable us to succeed in getting there. The last stop of our journey is Heaven and, if by hearing and listening to these messages we start praying better, if we start fasting, believing, being reconciled, forgiving, thinking of others, of helping them, we are doing well – this is the reaction of a Christian.

The source of our peace is the Lord and our hearts must become a source of peace; they must open up to the peace Our Lord gives.

In a message of about a month ago, Our Lady once again exhorted us to love our neighbour and said, « *Above all, those who provoke you* ». Here is where Christian love begins, that is to say, from peace.

Jesus said, « What is special in loving those who love you? In your forgiving those who forgive you? ». We must do more than that – we must love also the other one who causes us evil. Our Lady wants this – at this point peace starts, that is, when we start forgiving, being reconciled, unconditionally. In another message She said, « *Pray and love. Even those things that seem impossible to you become possible* ».

If any of us says, « How can I forgive? How can I be reconciled? », he has perhaps not yet asked for strength. Where should he look for it? From Our Lord, in prayer. If we have decided to live peace, reconciled with Our Lord and others, then peace starts, and the whole world is perhaps a milimetre closer to peace. Each of us who decides to live peace radically, by being reconciled, brings a new hope to the world; thus peace will come – if each one of us does not ask for peace from others, for love from others, but gives it readily himself.

What does conversion mean? It means not to allow oneself to give up trying to change. We all know our weaknesses and the weaknesses of others.

Think of Jesus' words when St. Peter asked, « How many times do we have to forgive? Seven times?». Peter thought seven times, but Jesus said, «Seventy times seven». One must on no account ever get tired of trying, but continue one's path with Our Lady.

In Her last Thursday's message, Our Lady said, «*I appeal to you, prepare yourselves for Christmas*», but you must prepare yourselves in prayer, penance, in works of love. «*Do not look at material things for they will stop you and you will not be able to live the experience of Christmas*». She repeated, as it were, all the messages – prayer, penance and works of love.

We have interpreted the messages in this way and in this way we try and live them in the community, in the parish – one hour for preparation, one hour for Mass, and after Mass, thanksgiving.

It is most important to pray in families, in the groups, in the parish; to pray and love as Our Lady said, and then all things, even those which seem impossible will become possible.

And when you get back to your homes, I wish you to try doing this. Everything can be changed for the better if we start praying, loving radically, unconditionally.

In order to love and pray this way, one must also pray for the grace of love.

Our Lady told us many times that Our Lord is happy if He can grant us His mercy, His love.

Also this evening He is at our disposal – and if we open ourselves, if we pray, Our Lord will grant us them.

(Fr. Slavko Barbarić - 7 December 1985)

Conversion lasts the whole of one's life

In my opinion, one very important thing for us all is what Our Lady asked Ivan's group a few weeks ago – to have a week's spiritual retreat, to have one wherever one happens to be, without looking for a cloister or a retreat house, but to hold one in our own daily life.

Each of us, especially now before Christmas, ought to spend a week this way, one ought to devote oneself more to prayer, more to silence, one ought to be more in contact with Our Lord; this programme is very beautiful and simple, suitable to us all. No matter where we are or what we do. What we can do is this – pray more at the beginning of the day, pray to the Holy Spirit, read the Bible, pray the Rosary, attend Mass. Let us retire and live one week this way.

Mirjana received a further apparition on 30 November – these messages, these words, all these things she heard and saw are an appeal to us. If we think of Jesus' parables where He was saying we must be awake, not asleep, we already have the answer to Mirjana's words.

The situation here with us is as follows: every day we see many people, many conversions, many healings, a new spirit of prayer, we receive a great many testimonies from all parts of the world. Many prayer groups are being created; many priests who have been here have decided – one day or one evening – to pray this way in their own parishes, together with their own people, as they have seen us do here, three hours of prayer. This is the most important thing. All those who have started to pray, to come together to pray in groups, in families, are doing well.

Prayer, fasting, faith, bring these events about in the face of all difficulties.

Last week, the Bishop's Commission had a new meeting – they have not decided anything. The next meeting will be held in May; they are allowing themselves some time for this, and this is a good thing.

Father Ivan, now working here at the Parish as chaplain and also a member of the Commission, has come back from the meeting more satisfied than usual – some seem to have noticed even the encouraging aspects. A member of the Commission told us, « Many say that the events of Medjugorje depend on the Franciscans. If the liturgy of Medjugorje belongs to the Franciscans, who do the Franciscans belong to? ». He meant, if this liturgy, if prayer and all that is happening is a work of theirs, then we know who they are.

It is most important for us to pray, to open ourselves to love, peace – all the rest will be given to us.

Conversion, in the messages of Medjugorje, means to change one's way of life, to forsake sin, selfishness, arrogance, pride, and to open ourselves to humility, love, and never to give up. Conversion has two elements – one, whereby we are called to forsake sin and another, whereby we are called to open ourselves to love. None of us will be able to say he loves enough, that he cannot love more. This is conversion – to try and love more, to try and get to be fully aware of sin, to pray for the spirit of love and to go forward.

I am saying this for the benefit of all those who have started with enthusiasm after hearing of the apparitions and have realised that change is not easy, it requires some hard work. Do not allow yourselves to tire, conversion lasts the whole of one's life. Our Lord understands this. Our Lady understands this – that is why She has invited all to confess every month. If She is inviting us to confession, one can say She knows we are sinners; She knows we will remain as such, but that does not matter. What matters is to look once again for reconciliation and the strength which is given to us by the Lord. This is hope and strength for us.

(Fr. Slavko Barbarić - 8 December 1985)

Our Lady wants us to start living our vocation radically

The admonishments and these messages have a simple meaning, they tell us nothing new, but simply bring us back to the Gospels before Christmas, to Jesus' words as to what is to happen – signs in the sky, in the stars, in the sun, earthquakes... Our Lady can say no more, but Her saying this should help our fear, our anguish, our new worries...

In what respect? Many Christians live saying, « I believe, I am a Christian, I go to church, I confess », but their hearts and lives are only on earth. Many say, « I believe », but rely on money, success, progress and material things alone and do not open themselves to the other things.

A true faith, a deep faith has this apocalyptic element – that is, I live my faith by my trust of the Lord; I know the Lord can call me any day.

We are wrong in saying. I shall be converted tomorrow, I shall forgive tomorrow, I shall be reconciled tomorrow; confession is asked of me today, not tomorrow.

So, the messages have this meaning – to be awake in faith, to work, to pray, to believe, to abandon oneself and be at the same time, open and ready everyday to be called and meet the Lord in love. Where do we stand now – you see that there are always many people coming here despite the winter. The message has been spread all over the world; I can honestly say Our Lady has found her agents everywhere.

One thing seems vital to me – next year has been declared « The Year of Peace » by UNESCO.

I do not know, but I think I can say that Medjugorje and all those who have started praying and fasting for peace, surely must have helped, if next year is to be declared the year of peace; and all those who have come to Medjugorje, all those who have read about Medjugorje, immediately will connect Medjugorje and the message of peace and many will be more open if there will be more talk of peace at all levels; it is probably a new chance for the whole world. And so we are all responsible for peace, most of all those who have accepted the message of the Queen of Peace. Praying for peace, fasting for peace and being reconciled with all those one lives with, that is how peace will come.

Peace does not come from treaties, it does not come from paper, peace comes from the heart of the man who lives peace and spreads peace, not just with words.

This kind of peace has justice, truth and love as its content. Where do wars come from? Why? Because many commit injustices and others do not forgive them – this is how conflicts in families, amongst people, in the Church and all over the world happen.

In other words – all those who start to live love for their neighbour and for God, all those who try and be righteous by also helping the poor, the needy, by so doing, pave the way for peace.

Many ask what stand is the government taking – all I can say is that we can work; you can come here and that is all. Something that seemed like a miracle to me was when, on 17 October, they showed a documentary film on Medjugorje on Belgrade Television; it was very good, it gave our people a fresh impulse. This is most important.

I say only one thing – in the Church, in the newspapers of the Church it is still forbidden to publish all that is happening here, but in this very situation you can see how God is behaving towards all of us.

God leaves us free and if we reject Our Lady, He finds somebody else; He finds the others, those who do not believe in God, who do not believe in Our Lady, but come here. These are wonderful things that help the spreading of the messages.

Here it seems to me, that the Word of the Lord has come true, when He said, « If you give praise to the Lord, the Lord can create a new descent from Abraham out of stones ».

It is a sign that Our Lady – as She once said in a message – is tireless. She will not leave us in peace until we will have found peace.

A priest told me, « I have guided two busloads to Medjugorje, I have felt more stimulus to prayer and faith than from all the work I have put in ». And he now often brings his people here and the number – he says – grows wonderfully all the time.

Another priest told me, « I asked my people to pray, but I did not pray myself. But when I did start to pray and confess every month, my parishioners did so too ».

Our Lady wants this – that we start living our vocation radically. We are all, and must be, apostles; we must spread peace; we are all equally invited to love. I wish you to really feel, during these days, the Lord's hand over you and also Our Lady's love and, thus blessed, may you go into the new year abandoned in prayer, living your lives in the love of your neighbour and God above all things.

(Fr. Slavko Barbarić - 27 December 1985)

« Abandon your hearts to me »

I only wish to talk briefly about the visionaries. There are still four of them who receive the daily apparitions – namely, Vicka, Marija, Jakov and Ivan.

Ivanka has not had any more apparitions since 7 May, the next one ought to occur on the anniversary of the apparitions, 25 June 1986. Mirjana has not been having daily apparitions since Christmas 1982, but has them for her birthday on 18 March and for the last few months she has been having internal locutions; she hears the same voice she used to hear during the apparitions and says Our Lady is talking to her mostly about the secrets and giving her new details.

During the two locutions of 25 October and 30 November Our Lady showed her, she says, the first admonishment, the first secret as in a film.

The admonishments, all Mirjana is telling us, must be understood in the context of the apparitions, that is, these rather apocalyptic messages forewarning that catastrophes are possible, a nuclear war is possible. But we know this to be true even without the apparitions. By coming to us, Our Lady wants to tell us that it is possible to find a path for peace once again. For this reason the apparitions are always a fact giving us renewed hope, they never want to give us anguish and fear, but always hope.

It is in this light that these admonishments must be interpreted; they do not occur because Our Lady is appearing, but Our Lady is appearing so that the horrible things we have been preparing for one another may be avoided. Mirjana said she will entrust a priest she confides in with the secrets ten days before their coming true, who in turn, will be able to tell the Parish and all those who want to hear them or are connected with Medjugorje, three days beforehand.

You know that prayer and fasting are two very important things in connection with these apparitions. Our Lady said, « *I am the Queen of Peace, I want to give you peace. Be reconciled, make peace* ». But all this can happen if we do our part and our part is to pray and fast, so that in prayer and fasting our own peace may also grow. Our Lord wants to give us peace if we pray, if we fast. Conversion, also, is another word for these apparitions, but conversion is given to us if we pray, if we fast.

In Her Thursday message after Christmas, She thanked all those who had lived the messages on Christmas Day. In two or three messages before Christmas, She also wanted to prepare us; in a message She said: « *Prepare yourselves for Christmas by prayer, penance and good works* ». These are a consequence of our conversion which must always be seen and measured against the Commandments of love towards God and our fellow men.

In another message before Christmas Our Lady said: « *Love your neighbour* », as a condition for being able to hear Jesus and « *If you abandon yourselves to Our Lord, the Father will bestow many graces on you* ». Our Lady promised her Maternal blessing to mothers.

So what was Our Lady asking of us before Christmas in order to enable us to glorify and praise Jesus and His birth on Christmas Day? She again asked for prayer, fasting and works of mercy. We do not know much about Our Lady's life, but it is certain that She prepared herself for her mission in this way too, in prayer, penance and works of mercy.

Before Christmas She said: « *If you abandon yourselves to Our Lord, he will give you many graces* » and thanked all those who had lived her messages and asked once more, « *Abandon your hearts to Me* ».

Before I even started to explain this, someone asked, « What does it mean to abandon oneself? ». I would say that to abandon oneself means to believe. You know that « believe » comes from « give with one's heart ».

To give with one's heart to someone means to trust someone, to trust in this sense – to entrust him with our past life, our present life, here and now, the present moment and also the future life, together with all the good things, and the bad things, with all our sins, with all our conflicts, to give Our Lord absolutely everything. If we do this, we can be healed from our sins, from the wounds we carry in us, in our hearts. To abandon oneself means to spend a lifetime with the Lord we love, and love is the condition necessary for us to be able to abandon ourselves.

Notice that, even in our human relationships, if we do not love someone, we cannot rely on him, we cannot open our hearts to him, we keep somewhat far away from him, at a distance.

When one gives one's heart it means – all I have, all I know, all I am, I give to you and you can do with it as you wish.

It is the same when engaged couples come to church and get married; holding hands, they say – look, I want to be with you always, even in difficult times, even in illness, forever, with you for the rest of my life. And the other one also says – I take you as my wife, as my husband and I am all for you. And if this is the true expression of love, then life becomes beautiful, it becomes full of joy and when troubles come they are easier to bear.

And if Our Lady says, « *Abandon your hearts to me* », it means – give everything to me, all your sufferings, all your weaknesses. Do not keep anything for yourselves, do not shut yourselves inside your anguish, your fears, but come out and trust the Lord. This abandonment can grow if we pray, if we fast, because by praying and fasting we will be given the experiences to enable us to take new steps towards Our Lord. So I will tell you once more – as your abandonment grows, so does « giving your heart », but unless you pray you cannot possibly experience such abandonment.

I have told you several times already – fast, fast.

You know Our Lady is asking for fasting twice a week – one must live on bread and water. If someone cannot, he can help himself with some tea or coffee, but in any case he ought to reduce material nourishment to the minimum. You can eat as much bread as you want, there is no limit, but it has to be bread alone. This fasting is

214

most important. If you read all the messages, you will see how many times Our Lady has asked us not to forget fasting.

Fasting, like prayer, is asked of us in the Bible. Fasting, together with prayer, helps faith, love. How?

By fasting we detach ourselves step by step from the material world and if we detach ourselves, we are given an inner grace, an inner freedom. By living this way, we are no longer attached to anything of this world and if we are not attached, we can more easily hear what the Lord has to say, what He wants from us.

And also in love, if we are more open to the Lord, the Lord will help us to love the others, to those we can help.

For this reason Our Lady is also asking for love for our neighbour, but She does not go into details, for each of us knows that, if he wants to live his love for his neighbour, he will find works of charity to be done according to his own capabilities, according to his own personal circumstances.

I say a rich man must fast, but that a poor man must also fast. Perhaps the first step a rich man will have to take is the one of sharing more with others. A poor man is not expected to give alms to the others; he is, however, expected to accept his poverty and from his own poverty, in his own poverty, to do good to the best of his ability.

This fasting is also vital for the Eucharist, for Mass. We have forgotten what it means to have our daily bread, for we have too many things and the more we have, the more discontented we became, but if we live on just bread for two days, we can see that we already have many things.

I have been gathering together a few experiences in these last few days; a girl told me, « I had many dresses and needed many clothes. Once, I do not know how, after having started to fast, I opened my wardrobe and saw – but with my heart – that I had far too many things; so many clothes hanging in my wardrobe all year long, which I may wear just once. At that very moment I understood I had to give them to others and I also found out how. After noticing I possessed too many things, which before I thought I needed and had to have, I understood something else – that I really did not need all those things I used to put on my face. The Lord has given me a nice face, why then waste so much money and so much time? And from that moment onwards I did not use anything any more ». A third experience, « Having given up these exterior things, attending Mass has become for me something wonderful. I sometimes feel that Jesus is not a little Host, but that Jesus is coming into my heart. So many times I feel so small that I wonder how God Almighty can possibly come into my heart ». And I believe that she really lives her faith and says, « I now feel, I now see, I now understand what it means to have enough, what it means to have a surplus. And what it means to be blind to what we have ».

Notice, this girl, I know her well, she has started to pray and fast radically; she knows her own troubles and her own crises, but she also knows her own wonderful path lying ahead.

This is what Our Lord wants from us – not that we are left without bread, without clothes, not that we do not work any more, but He wants to help us to see that we have enough.

This is the way, I repeat, to learn about abandonment; the sign that we are not abandoned to the Lord is our constant need for making this life secure for ourselves, our need for more.

Maybe some of you have heard of a book which has come out in Germany, « To have or to be. This is the alternative ». Some people only want to have, without wanting to be, in the sense of becoming a man, becoming a Christian. Here, by means of fasting, by means of prayer, Our Lord is giving us the right perspective, with regard to our life in this material world and to others. This is also the path to peace – if we become more righteous, if we live more completely the truth, more deeply the love for our neighbour, then peace will come.

Peace does not mean just lack of wars, but the fullness of physical, mental and spiritual gifts.

But what I am saying is just theory. What, instead, Our Lady has proposed we should do in order to obtain peace is a path – one must live it, one must start living it, step by step. Our Lady and Our Lord are cautious with us, they leave us time, they leave us to our own pace, but nevertheless want to guide us.

Even in Her last message of this year, Our Lady says, « *Abandon your hearts to Me* ». To mark this abandonment, Our Lady has asked us to meditate, every Thursday, the passage of St. Matthew's Gospel VI, 24-34, where Our Lord says, « Make up your minds, one cannot serve two masters, you will either love the one and hate the other ».

He then says, « Look at the birds, why allow yourselves to be distressed by worries? Look first of all for the Kingdom of God, all the rest will be granted unto you ».

If we understand this promise of Our Lord, much anguish, many fears, many aggressions will vanish and we will really be able to live in peace with ourselves, with God and also with others.

When one goes along this path with Our Lady, one also learns to be thankful. In a message She said that we must be thankful starting with the small things, in order to also be able to be thankful for the greater things.

To be thankful is another word for peace. Think of what it must be like in those families where the husband never says thank you to his wife, even for the smallest things. How will his wife feel? Awful. She will never take pleasure in doing things for her family, but if the others see what she does, if they notice particularly the small things, she will have more strength, more and more joy to carry on.

If children never notice what their parents do for them they will ask for more and if they ask for more, conflicts will come. But in order to be able to be thankful, one must learn of the many other things one learns in prayer and fasting.

One of these is humility. Humility means to let others live, to see the other person, to know him and not to use him as a tool, but to take him as a person.

I wish to say once again that one learns all these things as one goes along, step by step.

You know Our Lady has asked us to go regularly to confession. Somebody asked me to say something on how we should confess. When confessing, many people say, « I have not stolen, I have not hurt anybody, I have been praying a little, I have been attending Mass, I am a Christian ». All is in order.

It is not right to steal, it is not right to hurt others, that is true, and if we have done so we must confess it.

But this is rated as zero in Christian life. We are not Christians in order not to steal, not to hurt. We are Christians in order to do something positive, to love, to bring peace. I will give you an example: we do not have legs in order not to fall, but have legs to enable us to walk. Naturally we can fall, but we have the legs to go forward on. Similarily, we are Christians not to do no harm to others, but to act in a positive way to love, to bring peace. Therefore, it is not enough to say I did not steal, I did not swear; we must question ourselves on our positive actions and realise whether we have been doing what we were supposed to; if we have in effect loved others, if we have brought peace, comfort, if we have been sharing with others.

I am telling you, that if you start with a deeper spiritual life, you will feel even the smallest things that need to be confessed. I am not saying you should become full of scruples; no, I am not, but when one leads a deeper spiritual life, one can understand better, one senses injustices better, one can get a better sense of all those opportunities where we could have done some good. So, confess always what you feel was not right, but also look positively at what people may have been expecting of you.

If one goes ahead, one will see new things. Just today I have been dealing with a very interesting case – a girl, who had been here for almost three months and was living a really intense life of prayer, and yet felt that she was making no progress, said, « I have been praying to Jesus; tell me, what is still stopping me from being totally open? ». The answer was, « Your relationship with your mother ». She could not understand. She asked, « How is that? I forgave my mother ». But when she began to ask herself once more, she discovered an obstacle within herself, a real obstacle, and I am most certain, for I know her well, that this is the thing that needs to come out of her heart before she is able to totally abandon herself.

But, mind you, as you go ahead, you tend to discover things and as I have already told you, Our Lord is very cautious with us. I happen to know that if the girl had experienced this perhaps three months ago, she may not have understood everything, but she only slowly became aware at the right moment and is now able to go on.

Many people who have started to live a deeper life, often sense these things. A boy who became converted here told me, « My life is now a little more difficult than before. Before, I used to be pleased with myself; now I am not, now I see my capacities, but also my duties, they do not scare me, but I see I must do more ». I said, « Look, when you give your hand to the Lord, the Lord leads you forward ». We are sometimes somewhat inert and quite happy to say, « I have done no harm to anybody ». I repeat, this is worth zero. Think of St. Francis, the day before he died, he said, « My dear brothers, let us start afresh, we have not yet done anything ». It is not true that he had not done anything; on the contrary, he had done a lot, and the Church and the entire world acknowledge him as a great saint, yet he said, « We have not done anything », this is the sentiment of a saint.

I tell our priests that when they confess here, they ought to confess and look beyond confession. For example, it is not enough to say, « I go to Mass on Sunday ». It is not enough here – if Our Lady is asking for a preparation to Mass, every priest ought to discuss with those who come to confession, and ask them whether they prepare themselves for Mass.

Just to give you an example, look at what is happening in many places, perhaps everywhere. One comes to Church when the bells are ringing and, as soon as one receives the blessing, one walks out. If you arrive at the church a little tired and irritable because you have been looking for a parking space, what can you hope to receive from Mass, which is only forty or fifty minutes long? In a kitchen where the best foods are prepared so that they can be eaten, if one does not eat, one dies of starvation. So why do so many people not go to Mass anymore? Because they did not prepare themselves for Mass, they did not receive anything and then asked themselves, « Why go? Why go if I get nothing out of it? ».

Hence one ought to prepare oneself and make one's thanksgiving. What does it mean to prepare oneself? For example, to arrive some twenty minutes earlier and pray a little, a Rosary, for example, something, and rest close to Our Lord. What does it mean to make our thanksgiving – for instance, we here pray for the sick. but this prayer is always for us all and we start by repeating to the living Jesus received in the Host, « You, O Lord have the Word for me, You can heal me ». But how can Jesus heal us if we do not allow Him to heal us, if we go out straightaway, if we run away immediately? So, therefore, let us take a little more time before and after Mass and in this way we will be able to go forward.

(Fr. Slavko Barbarić - 30 December 1985)

THE MESSAGES OF OUR LADY
TO THE PARISH OF MEDJUGORJE*

1st March, 1984

Dear children, I have chosen this Parish in a special way and wish to guide it. I will protect it with my love and wish that all of you may belong to me. Thank you for having answered my call this evening. I look forward to ever greater numbers of you joining me and my Son. Every Thursday I will give you a special message.

8th March, 1984

Thank you for your response to my call. All of you in this Parish, dear children, be converted. This is my second wish; in this way you will help to convert all those who come here.

15th March, 1984

I am particularly grateful also this evening because you have come, dear children. Continue the Adoration of the Blessed Sacrament. I am always present when the faithful are in adoration. This is the moment in which to receive special gifts.

22rd March, 1984

Dear children. I invite you this evening to honour, particularly during Lent, the sacred wounds of my Son which have been inflicted because of the sins of this Parish. Join me in prayer for the Parish so that His suffering may be alleviated.
Thank you for your response to my call. Try to come always in greater numbers.

* Text translated from the Croat.

29th March, 1984

Dear children. I urge you this evening to be particularly persevering during trials. Reflect on how the Omnipotent suffers to-day on account of your sins. Offer your sufferings to God. Thank you for your response to my call.

5th April, 1984

Dear children. This evening I ask you especially to honour the Heart of my Son Jesus. Think of the sacred wounds caused to the Heart of my Son, that Heart hurt by so many sins. Thank you for having come also this evening.

12th April, 1984

Dear children. To-day I ask you to stop all the tittle-tattle and to pray for the unity of the Parish, because both my Son and I have a special plan for this Parish.
Thank you for your response to my call.

19th April, 1984

Dear children. Have compassion on me. Pray, pray, pray.

26th April, 1984

Our Lady did not give any message.

3rd May, 1984

The visionary, Marija, asked Our Lady: « Dear Mother, why did you not give the message for the Parish last Thursday? »
To which the Virgin replied: « I do not wish to force anybody to do anything they do not feel or wish to do, even if I had some special message to give to the Parish with which I wanted to revive the faith of all the faithful. Only very few of you have accepted the Thursday messages. To start with there were many more of you. Unfortunately, for many of you it has become something quite common place and lately some were only asking for the message out of curiosity and not out of faith or devotion towards my Son and I. »

10th May, 1984

Many faithful appear to be struck by the last message of Our Lady. Some thought that the Blessed Virgin would not have given any more a message for the Parish, but this evening She said: « I will speak to you because I wish to tell you more. Try to pay attention to my advice. »

17th May, 1984

Dear children. To-day I am very happy as there are so many people who wish to consecrate themselves to me. Thank you. You have not been misled. My Son Jesus Christ wishes, through me, to give you special gifts; my Son is happy for your abandonment.
Thank you for your response to my call.

24th May, 1984

Dear children. I have already told you that I have chosen you in a very special way, just as you are. I, your Mother, love all of you so do not be afraid in moments of difficulty. I love you even when you are far from me and my Son. I beg of you, do not allow my Heart to cry tears of blood for the souls who lose themselves in sin; for this, dear children, pray, pray.
Thank you for your response to my call.

31st May, 1984 (Feast of the Ascension)

There were many people present. Our Lady did not give the message for the Parish and told the visionary Marija that she would give the message next Saturday so that it could be announced on Sunday during the 11 o'clock Mass.

2nd June, 1984

Dear children. This evening I wish to tell you that during this Novena you should pray for the Holy Spirit to descend on your families and on the Parish. Pray. You will not regret it. God will give you those gifts with which you will glorify Him until the end of your earthly lives.

9th June, 1984

Dear children. To-morrow evening please pray for the Holy Spirit of Truth, especially you of this Parish, because you need the Spirit of Truth in order to transmit the messages exactly and faithfully as they are given to you, without adding or taking anything away. Pray so that the Holy Spirit may inspire you with the Spirit of prayer, so that you may pray more. I, your Mother, tell you that you pray very little.

Thank you for your response to my call.

14th June, 1984

No special message was given.

21st June, 1984

Pray, pray, pray.

Thank you for your response to my call.

28th June, 1984

There was no special message for the Parish.

5th July, 1984

Dear children. To-day I wish to tell you that you should pray before you start any work and that you should finish your work with prayer. If you do so, God will bless you and your work. In these days you are working a lot and praying little. Therefore, pray: you will rest in prayer. Thank you for your response to my call.

12th July, 1984

Dear children. In these days satan wants to hinder my plans. Please pray so that his plan may not be realized. I will pray to my Son Jesus so that He may give you the grace to feel the victory of Jesus in the trials inflicted upon you by satan.

Thank you for your response to my call.

224

19th July, 1984

Dear children. In these days you have experienced the work of satan. I am always with you, so do not be afraid of the trials, as God always watches over us. I have given myself to you and share with you even the smallest trial.
Thank you for your response to my call.

26th July, 1984

Dear children. To-day again, I wish to invite you to persevere in your prayer and in penance; especially the young people of this Parish should take a more active part in their prayers.
Thank you for your response to my call.

2nd August, 1984

Dear children. To-day I am happy and thank you for your prayers. Pray still more in these days for the conversion of sinners.
Thank you for your response to my call.

9th August, 1984

Dear children. Please pray as satan wants to impede my plans again. Pray with your hearts and abandon yourselves in prayer to Jesus.

16th August, 1984

Dear children. I ask you in particular, of this Parish, to live my messages and to transmit them to all you meet.
Thank you for your response to my call.

23rd August, 1984

Pray, pray, pray (Marija says that the faithful and, in particular, the young people were called to order during Mass).

30th August, 1984

Dear children. The cross was part of the Divine plan when it was

built. Go to-day to the mountain and pray under the cross. I need your prayers.
Thank you for your response to my call.

6th September, 1984

Dear children. Without your prayers there is no peace. This is why I say: dear children, pray under the cross for peace.
Thank you for your response to my call.

13th September, 1984

Dear children. I still need your prayers. You will ask yourselves: why so many prayers? Look around you, dear children, and you will see how immense is the sin which reigns on this earth. Please pray, therefore, so that Jesus may win.
Thank you for your response to my call.

20th September, 1984

Dear children. To-day I urge you to begin your fasting with all your heart. There are already many of you who fast, more than anything else because everybody fasts, and so it has become a habit that nobody wants to break. I ask the Parish, please fast in order to thank God for having allowed me to stay in this Parish for so long. Dear children, fast and pray with your hearts.
Thank you for your response to my call.

27th September, 1984

Dear children. You have helped me with your prayers so that my plans may be fulfilled. Please continue to pray so that all my plans may be carried out. I commend all families of this Parish to recite the Rosary.
Thank you for your response to my call.

4th October, 1984

Dear children. To-day I wish to tell you that you have made me ever so happy by your prayers, even though there are still many in the Parish who do not yet pray and for whom my heart is sad. Pray, to enable me to bring all your sacrifices and your prayers to the Lord.

Thank you for your response to my call.

11th October, 1984

Dear children. Thank you for having dedicated all your labour to God, even though He is now putting you to the test by the fruits that you are gathering in these days. You must know, dear children, that He loves you and is therefore testing you. You must always entrust all your burdens to God and you must not worry about anything.

Thank you for your response to my call.

18th October, 1984

Dear children. To-day I call you that you should read the Holy Bible in your homes every day. It should be placed in a prominent place where it can always be seen and where it reminds you that it « must be read » and accompanied by prayer.

Thank you for your response to my call.

25th October, 1984

Dear children. Please pray during this month. God has permitted me to help you every day and to defend you from evil. This is my month. I want to give it to you. You only have to pray to God and God will give you what you ask. And I will help you.

Thank you for your response to my call.

1st November, 1984

Dear children. To-day I urge you to renew your prayer in your homes. Your work has finished. You must now devote yourselves to prayer. Prayer should be at the first place in your families.

Thank you for your response to my call.

8th November, 1984

Dear children. You are not aware of the messages that God is sending you through me. He is granting you great gifts that you do not understand. Pray so that the Holy Spirit may illuminate you. If you only realized the extent of mercy that God is bestowing upon you, you would pray without ceasing.

Thank you for your response to my call.

15th November, 1984

Dear children. You are the chosen ones and God bestows on you great mercy. You are not able to understand every message that I am giving you. Now, I only want to say: pray, pray, pray. I do not know what else to say because I love you and wish that through prayer you may be in a position to feel my love and the love of God.

Thank you for your response to my call.

22nd Novembre, 1984

Dear children. In these days you must live all the main messages and root them in your hearts until next Thursday.

Thank you for your response to my call.

29th November, 1984

Dear children. No, you do not know how to love and you do not know how to listen to what I say with love. You must be conscious, my loved ones, that I am your Mother and that I have come on this earth to teach you to listen with love and to pray with love but not forcibly, so that you can bear the cross. God is glorified through all men by the cross.

Thank you for your response to my call.

6th December, 1984

Dear children. In these days I call you to prayer in your families. In the name of God I have given you the messages many times, but you have not listened. This Christmas will be unforgettable for you, only if you will accept the messages that I am giving you. Dear Children, do not let the day of joy become a day of sorrow for me.

Thank you for your response to my call.

13th December, 1984

Dear children. You know that the time of joyfulness is near and that without love you will be unable to achieve anything. So, the first thing you must do is to love your family, all in the Parish, and only then will you be able to accept and to love all who come here. Dedicate this week, then, to learn how to love.

Thank you for your response to my call.

20th December, 1984

Dear children. To-day I am calling you to do something positive for Jesus. I would like every family in the Parish to bring a flower every day until the day of Joy, as a sign of abandonment to Jesus. I would like every member to place a flower beside the crib so that Jesus may come and see your abandonment to Him.

Thank you for your response to my call.

27th December, 1984

Dear children. This Christmas satan wanted very much to upset God's plans. You, dear children, must have felt the presence of satan also on Christmas Day. But God won in all your hearts. And may happiness reign in your hearts.

Thank you for your response to my call.

3rd January, 1985

Dear children. During these days the Lord has given you great graces. I would like, therefore, that this week be a week of thanks for all the graces you have received from the Lord.
Thank you for your response to my call.

10th January, 1985

Dear children. To-day, again I would like to thank you for all your offerings, in particular I thank those who are dear to my heart and who come here willingly. There are still many parishioners who do not hear the messages, but because of those who are specially dear to me, for their sake, I will continue to give the messages to the Parish. And I will still give them because I love you and want you to spread the messages with your heart.
Thank you for your response to my call.

17th January, 1985

In these days satan is perfidiously battling against your Parish. And you, dear children, have gone to sleep with your prayers and only a few of you go to Mass. Be strong in days of temptation.
Thank you for your response to my call.

24th January, 1985

Dear children. In these days you have experienced the grace of God through the renewals occurring in this Parish. Satan, always fiercer, wants to steal your joy from you. With your prayers you can completely disarm him and ensure your happiness.
Thank you for your response to my call.

31st January, 1985

Dear children. To-day I wish to tell you to open your hearts to God as the flowers of Spring seek the sun: I am your Mother and always want you to be nearer to the Father so that He may always offer many gifts to your hearts.
Thank you for your response to my call.

7th Fabruary, 1985

Dear children. In these days satan has been very much in evidence in this Parish. Please pray, my dear ones, so that the will of God may be done and that every action of satan may end in the glory of God. I have stayed so long in order to help you to resist the temptations.

Thank you for your response to my call.

14th February, 1985

Dear children. To-day is the day that I come to give you the message but not all the Parish accepts the messages and lives them. I am sad and would like you, dear children, to listen to them and live my messages. Every family must pray united and read the Bible.

Thank you for your response to my call.

21st February, 1985

Dear children. Day after day I ask you to renew your prayer in the Parish, but you do not comply. To-day I am calling you for the last time. It is now Lent and you as a Parish are now able to respond to my call with love. Should you not do so I will not give you the messages any more. This is granted to me by God.

Thank you for your response to my call.

28th February, 1985

Dear children. To-day I invite you to live, during this coming week, the words: I love God. Dear children, with love, you can do anything, even that which you may think impossible. God would like this Parish to belong entirely to Him. I too wish the same.

Thank you for your response to my call.

7th March, 1985

Dear children. To-day I invite you to renew your prayer in your families. Dear children. Stimulate the others to prayer and even the smallest ones to go to Mass.

Thank you for your response to my call.

14th March, 1985

Dear children. Each one of you has experienced the light and the darkness in your lives. God gives everyone the discernment to know good and evil. I invite you to the light which you must bring to all those who live in darkness. Day after day people who live in darkness come to your homes. Show them, dear children, the light. Thank you for your response to my call.

21st March, 1985

Dear children. I want to give you the messages and invite you therefore to-day, to live and accept my messages. Dear children. I love you and have chosen this Parish which is especially dear to me and where I love to be since Almighty God sent me. This is why I invite you, dear children, so that you may also have greater blessings. Listen to my messages.
Thank you for your response to my call.

24th March, 1985 (Eve of the Feast of the Annunciation)

Dear children. To-day I invite you to go to confession, even if you have already been only a few days ago. I want you to be able to live my Feast Day in your hearts, but you cannot live it if you do not abandon yourself to the Lord, so I invite you: « Be reconciled to the Lord. »

28th March, 1985

Dear children. To-day I want to invite you to: pray, pray, pray. In prayer you will discover the most sublime joy and the answer to all your problems which may seem impossible. Thank you for having started to pray. In my heart everyone is somebody special and I thank you who have encouraged their families to pray.
Thank you for your response to my call.

4th April, 1985 (Maundy Thursday)

Dear children. I thank you for having begun to think more of the joy of God in your hearts. It was to-day that I had intended to stop giving you the messages because some of you were not accepting me. But the Parish has acted, so I want to continue giving you the messages in a way that has never happened in history, from the beginning of the world.

Thank you for your response to my call.

11th April, 1985

Dear children. To-day I wish to say to all the Parish: pray in a very special way so that the Holy Spirit may enlighten you. To-day God wishes to put the Parish to the test in a very particular way in order to strengthen its faith.

Thank you for your response to my call.

18th April, 1985

Dear children. To-day I thank you for every opening of your hearts. I am full of joy for every heart that opens itself to the Lord, especially for those among the Parish. Rejoice with me. Pray so that the hearts which are under the burden of sin may open up. I so desire it. Through me the Lord wishes it so.

I thank you because you have followed my call.

26th April, 1985

Dear children. To-day I wish to say to you: begin to cultivate your hearts in the way you cultivate your fields. Cultivate and change your hearts so that the new Spirit of God may dwell in your hearts.

Thank you because you have followed my call.

2nd May, 1985

Dear children. To-day I invite you to pray with your hearts and not as a routine. Some of you have come, but do not want to go deeply into the prayer of the heart. As a mother, I invite you: pray so that prayer may prevail in your hearts in every situation.

Thank you because you have followed my call.

9th May, 1985

Dear children. You do not know what great graces the Lord gives you. You do not want to stir yourselves in these days during which the Holy Spirit is at work in a special way. Your hearts are concerned with earthly goods and these goods are troubling you. May your hearts be converted towards prayer and ask the Holy Spirit to descend on you.

Thank you because you have followed my call.

16th May, 1985
Dear children. I call you to a more active prayer and also to participate at Holy Mass. I want the Holy Mass to become an experience of God for you. I specially wish to tell the young: be open to the Holy Spirit because God wants to bring you closer to Him in these days when satan is very active.

I thank you because you have responded to my call.

23rd May, 1985
Dear children. I invite you specially in these days to open your hearts to the Holy Spirit. In these days, in particular, the Holy Spirit is working through you. Open your hearts and offer your lives to Jesus so that He may work through your hearts and strengthen you in your faith.

Thank you because you have responded to my call.

30th May, 1985
Dear children. I call on you again to pray with the heart. Dear children, may prayer become your daily nourishment, specially now that your work in the fields takes up so much time and you are unable to pray with the heart. Pray and you will overcome all tiredness. Prayer will be both joy and rest for you.

Thank you because you have responded to my call.

6th June, 1985
Dear children. In these next days men from all nations will come to this Parish. And I now invite you to love: above all, love your

relatives and only then will you be able to accept and love all those who come to you.
Thank you because you have followed my call.

13th June, 1985

Dear children. From now until the fourth anniversary, I ask you to pray more in the Parish and to abandon yourselves still more in prayer to God. Dear children, I know that you are tired because you still cannot abandon yourselves to me. Abandon yourselves to me completely in these next days.
Thank you for your response to my call.

20th June, 1985

Dear children. For this Feast I want to say to you: «Open your hearts to the Lord of all hearts.» Give all your feelings and all your problems to me. I want to comfort you in your temptations. I want to fill you with peace, the joy and the love of God.
Thank you for your response to my call.

25th June, 1985

I invite you all to recite the Rosary. With the Rosary you will overcome all evil that satan now intends to inflict on the Catholic Church. May the priests recite the Rosary. Dedicate your time to the reciting of the Rosary. (Our Lady gave this message to the visionary Marija Pavlovic in answer to her question: «Blessed Virgin, what would you like to say to priests?»).

28th June, 1985

Dear children. With to-day's message I want to invite you to humility. In these days you have felt a great joy for all the people who have come here, and with love you have shared your experiences with them. I now ask you to continue in humility and with an open heart to talk to all those who come here.
Thank you for your response to my call.

4th July, 1985

Dear children. I thank you for every sacrifice you have offered. Now I want to urge you to offer every sacrifice with love and abandonment. I desire that you, who are weak, begin helping trustfully and Our Lord will give you his trust in return.
Thank you for your response to my call.

11th July, 1985

Dear children. I love this parish and protect it with my cloak from every work of satan. Pray that satan may flee from this parish and every individual who comes to this parish. In this way you will be able to hear every call of God, and answer with your life.
Thank you for your response to my call.

18th July, 1985

Dear children. Today I invite you to put more blessed objects in your home and everyone of you to carry some blessed objects on them. Let all the things be blessed so that satan will tempt you less because you have an armour against him.
Thank you for your response to my call.

25th July, 1985

Dear children. I want to guide you, but you do not want to listen to my messages. Today I ask you to listen to my messages and then you will be able to live everything that God tells me to transmit to you. Open yourselves to God, and God will be able to act through you and give you everything you need.
Thank you for your response to my call.

1st August, 1985

Dear children. I wish to tell you that I have chosen this parish and I hold it in my hands, caring for it like a flower that does not want to die. I invite you to abandon yourselves to me so that I am able to give you to God, pure and immaculate. Satan has taken part of my plan and wants to make it his own. Pray that he may not succeed, because I want you all for myself so that I may offer you to God.

Thank you for your response to my call.

8th August, 1985

Dear children. Today I particularly invite you to engage yourselves in the fight against satan by means of prayer. Satan acts more aggressively now that you are aware of his action. Dear children, take up your arms against satan and defeat him with the Rosary in your hands.

Thank you for your response to my call.

15th August, 1985

Dear children. Today I bless you and wish to tell you I love you, and I urge you to live my messages. Today I bless you all with the solemn blessing that the Almighty has granted me.

Thank you for your response to my call.

22nd August, 1985

Dear children. Today I wish to tell you that God wants to put you to the test; you can overcome these tests with prayer. God tests you through the work of every day. Now pray in order to overcome each of these tests calmly. Through all these difficulties Our Lord gives you, open yourselves more and more to God each day and go towards Him with love.

Thank you for your response to my call.

29th August, 1985

Dear children. I am calling you to prayer, especially now when satan wants to make use of the grapes of your vineyards. Pray that he may not succeed in his plan.

Thank you for your response to my call.

5th September, 1985

Dear children. Today I thank you for all the prayers. Continue praying all the more, so that satan will be driven from this place. Dear children, satan's plan has failed. Pray for the fulfilment of all that God is planning for this parish. I thank the young people especially for the sacrifices they have offered.
Thank you for your response to my call.

12th September, 1985

Dear children. I wish to tell you that, at this time, the Cross must be the centre. Pray especially before the Cross from which many graces are coming. Make a special consecration to the Cross in your homes. Promise that you will not offend Jesus in the Cross and that you will not blaspheme.
Thank you for your response to my call.

19th September, 1985

Dear children. Today I am calling you to live the messages I give you with humility. Dear children, do not become proud because you are living the messages. Do not go around saying « we are living them ». If you bear the messages in your heart and live them, everyone will feel it. So words will not be necessary, and are being used only by those who do not listen. You do not have to speak with words. You, dear children, have to live and witness with your lives.
Thank you for your response to my call.

26th September, 1985

Dear children. I thank you for all your prayers. I thank you for all your sacrifices. I wish to tell you, dear children, to renew the messages I am giving you. Live the fasting especially, because with fasting you will succeed in fulfilling God's plan here in Medjugorje. Thus you give me great joy.
Thank you for your response to my call.

3rd October, 1985

Dear children. I want to tell you to thank God for all the graces He has given you. Thank God, and give Him glory for all the fruits. Dear children, learn to give thanks for little things and then you will be able to give thanks for the big things.

Thank you for your response to my call.

10th October, 1985

Dear children. Also today I want to call you to live the messages in the parish. I want especially to call the young of my dear parish. Dear children, if you live the messages, you live the seed of holiness too. As Mother, I want to call all of you to holiness, so that you are able to give it to others. You are a mirror to others.

Thank you for your response to my call.

17th October, 1985

Dear children. Everything has its own time. Today I am calling you to start working on your hearts. Now that work in the fields has ended, you find time for cleaning the most neglected areas, but you leave your hearts aside. Work more, and clean every part of your heart with love.

Thank you for your response to my call.

24th October, 1985

Dear children. From day to day I wish to clothe you in sancity, goodness, obedience and divine love, so that from day to day you may become more pure and more ready for your Lord. Dear children, listen to, and live, my messages. I want to lead you.

Thank you for your response to my call.

31st October, 1985

Dear children. Today I want to call you to work in the Church. I love all of you equally, and I want everyone to work according to their capabilities. I know, dear children, that you are able to, but you do not do so because you do not feel capable of it. You must be courageous, and offer little flowers to the Church and to Jesus, so that all may be pleased.

Thank you for your response to my call.

7th November, 1985

Dear children. I am calling you to love your fellow men; above all, to love those who cause you evil. In that way, you will be able, with love, to value your hearts' intentions. Pray and love. Dear children, with love even impossible things become possible.

Thank you for your response to my call.

14th November, 1985

Dear children. I, your Mother, love you and wish to urge you continuously to prayer. Dear children, I am tireless and I call you even when you are far from my heart. I am your Mother, and though I feel sorrow for anyone who goes astray, I forgive easily and I rejoice for every child who comes back to me.

Thank you for your response to my call.

21st November, 1985

Dear children. I wish to tell you that this is a special time for you of the parish. You say that you have a lot of work in summer. Now there is no work in the fields and, for this reason, I ask you to work on yourselves, personally. Come to Mass, because this time is given to you. Dear children, there are many who come regularly in spite of the bad weather, because they love me and want to show their love for me. I ask all of you to show me your love by coming to Mass, and the Lord will reward you generously.

Thank you for your response to my call.

28th November, 1985

Dear children. I want to thank everyone for all they have done

for me. I especially wish to thank the young people. I beg you, dear children, dedicate yourselves to prayer with awareness and, in this way, in prayer you will know the glory of Our Lord.
Thank you for your response to my call.

5th December, 1985

Dear children. I call you to prepare yourselves for Christmas with penance, prayer and works of love. Dear children, do not worry yourselves too much about material things or you will not be able to live the feast of Christmas.
Thank you for your response to my call.

12th December, 1985

Dear children. This Christmas I invite you to give glory to Jesus with me. On that day I offer Him to you in a special way. I invite you to glorify Jesus and his birth. Dear children, pray more, and think more about Jesus on that day.

19th December, 1985

Dear children. Today I want especially to invite you to love your neighbour. If you love your neighbour you will experience Jesus more, particularly at Christmas. God will bestow great gifts upon you if you abandon yourselves to Him. For Christmas I particularly want to give mothers my own special blessing. Jesus will bless everyone else.
Thank you for your response to my call.

26th December, 1985

Dear children. I want to thank all of you who have listened to my messages, and who have lived Christmas Day as I asked you. Cleansed of your sins, from now on I want to lead you in love. Abandon your hearts to me.
Thank you for your response to my call.

PRAYERS

Prayer of Consecration to the Sacred Heart of Jesus *

Jesus, we know that You are merciful
and that You have offered Your heart for us.
It is crowned with thorns and with our sins.
We know that You implore us constantly
so that we do not go astray.
Jesus, remember us
when we are in sin.
By means of Your Heart
make all men love one another.
Make hate disappear from amongst men.
Show us Your love.
We all love You
and want You to protect us
with Your Shepherd's Heart and free us from every sin.
Jesus, enter into every heart!
Knock, knock at the door of our heart.
Be patient and never desist.
We are still closed
because we have not understood Your Love.
Knock continuously.
O Good Jesus, make us open our hearts to You
at least in the moment we remember Your
Passion suffered for us. Amen.

* Dictated by Our Lady to Jelena Vasilj, 28th November, 1983.

Consecration to the Immaculate Heart of Mary *

O Immaculate Heart of Mary, ardent with goodness,
show Your Love towards us.
May the flame of Your Heart, O Mary,
descend on all mankind.
We love You so.
Impress true love in our hearts
so that we have a continuous desire
for You.
O Mary, humble and meek of heart,
remember us when we are in sin.
You know that all men sin.
Give us, by means of Your Immaculate Heart,
spiritual health.
Let us always see
the goodness of Your Maternal Heart
and may we be converted by means of the flame
of Your Heart. Amen.

* Dictated by Our Lady to Jelena Vasilj, 28th November, 1983.

Prayer to the Mother of Goodness, Love and Mercy [*]

O Mother mine,
Mother of goodness, love and mercy,
I love you infinitely
and I offer myself to You.
By means of Your goodness, Your love
and Your grace, save me.
I desire to be Yours.
I love you infinitely,
and desire You to protect me.
From the depth of my heart I pray You, Mother of goodness,
give me Your goodness.
Let me gain Heaven by means of it.
I pray you, by Your infinite love,
to give me the grace,
so that I may love every man,
as You have loved Jesus Christ.
I pray You to give me the grace
to be merciful towards You. [**]
I offer myself to You completely and desire
that You follow my every step.
Because You are full of grace.
And I desire that I will never forget this.
And if, by chance, I should lose grace
I pray you to restore it to me once more. Amen.

[*] Dictated by Our Lady to Jelena Vasilj, 19th April, 1983.
[**] The phrase « I pray you to give me the grace to be merciful towards you »
means « Give me the grace to love your will which is different to mine ».

Supplication to God *

« O God,
our heart is in deep darkness;
in spite of this it is bound to Your Heart.
Our heart struggles between You and satan;
do not allow this to be so!

And every time our heart is divided
between good and evil
may it be illuminated by Your light
and made whole.

Never allow
two loves to dwell within us,
or that two faiths may ever co-exist,
and never allow to dwell amongst us:
falsehood and sincerity,
love and hate,
honesty and dishonesty,
humility and pride.

Rather, help us
so that our heart may rise up to You like that of a child,
Let our heart be captured by peace
and may it ever continue to feel nostalgia for it.

May Your holy will and Your love
find their abode in us,
that at least some times we desire truly to be Your children.

* The visionary Jelena Vasilj says that Our Lady dictated this prayer to her
on 22nd June, 1985 and advised her to recite it in the prayer group.

And when, Lord,
we do not wish to be Your children,
remember our past desires
and help us to receive You once more.

We open our hearts to You
so that Your holy love may dwell in them;
we open our souls to You
so that they may be touched by Your holy mercy,
which will help us to see all our sins clearly
and will make us understand
that what renders us impure is sin!

O God, we wish to be Your children,
so humble and devoted
as to become dear and sincere children,
as only the Father
could wish us to be.

Help us, Jesus, our brother,
to obtain the forgiveness of the Father **
and help us to be good towards Him ***
Help us, Jesus,
to understand clearly what God gives us
because sometimes we give up doing a good deed
believing it to be a wrong. »

_____

After this prayer, recite the Glory Be three times.

** Literally « to appease Your Father towards us. »
*** Jelena related later that Our Lady explained the meaning of this verse
thus:
« So that He may mercifully make goodness come back to us and so make
us good. »
It is the same thing as when a small child says: « Brother, tell Father to be
good, because I love him, and so I too may be good towards him. »

Prayer for the sick *

O my God,
this sick person here before You
has come to ask You
what he desires, and
what he believes to be the most important thing for himself.

Grant, O God,
that these words enter into his heart:
« It is important to be healthy in the soul! »

Lord,
May Your holy will
be done unto him in everything!
If you wish that he be healed
may he be given health.
But if Your will is different
may he continue to bear his cross.

I pray to You also for us
who intercede for him;
purify our hearts
so as to make us worthy
for Your holy mercy to be given through us.

* During the apparition of 22nd June, 1985, the visionary Jelena Vasilj says
that Our Lady said this about the Prayer for the Sick: « Dear Children. The
most beautiful prayer you are able to recite for a sick person is really this
one! »
Jelena asserts that Our Lady declared that Jesus Himself recommended it.
Jesus wishes that the sick person and also those who intercede with the prayer
be entrusted into the hands of God.

Protect him and relieve his sufferings,
may Your holy will be done unto him.

Through him may Your holy name be revealed:
help him to bear his cross with courage.

After this prayer, recite the Glory Be three times.

The Lord's Prayer

Our Lady teaches the Lord's Prayer to the prayer group* and wishes that this prayer be understood in this way:

FATHER

- Who is this Father?
- whose is this Father?
- where is this Father?

OUR

- this is your Father
- why are you afraid of Him?
- hold out your hands to Him.

.... (make a short pause)

OUR FATHER means that He has given Himself to you as Father, He has given you everything. You know that your earthly fathers do everything for you, so much more does your Heavenly Father.

OUR FATHER means: I give you everything, my child.

WHO ART IN HEAVEN

FATHER WHO ART IN HEAVEN

.... (make a short pause)

This means: Your earthly father loves you, but your Heavenly Father loves you even more. Your Father can get angry: He does not; He offers you only love...

---

* Through Jelena Vasilj.

HALLOWED BE THY NAME

In exchange you must respect Him, because He has given you everything and because He is your Father and you must love Him. You must glorify and praise His name. You must say to sinners: He is the Father; yes, He is my Father and I wish to serve Him and to glorify only His name. This is the meaning of «HALLOWED BE THY NAME».

THY KINGDOM COME

This is how we thank Jesus and mean to tell Him: Jesus, we know nothing, without Your Kingdom we are weak, if You are not present together with us. Our kingdom passes, whilst Yours does not pass away. Re-establish it!

THY WILL BE DONE

O Lord, make our kingdom collapse, let Your Kingdom be the only true one, and make us realise that our kingdom is destined to end and that at once, NOW, we allow Thy will to be done.

ON EARTH AS IT IS IN HEAVEN

Here, Lord, it is said how the angels obey you, how they respect you; let us be like them too, let our hearts open too and may they respect You like the angels do now. And make it possible for everything on earth to be Holy as it is in Heaven.

GIVE US THIS DAY OUR DAILY BREAD

Give us, Lord, bread and food for our soul; give it to us now, give it to us today, give it to us always; that this bread may become food for our soul, may nourish us, may that bread sanctify You, may that bread become eternal.

O Lord, we pray to you for our bread. O Lord, let us receive it. O Lord, help us to understand what we must do.

Let us realise that our daily bread cannot be given to us without prayer.

AND FORGIVE US OUR TRESPASSES

Forgive us Lord our trespasses. Forgive us them because we are not good and we are not faithful.

AS WE FORGIVE THEM THAT TRESPASS AGAINST US

Forgive us them so that we too may forgive those we were not capable of forgiving until now.

O Jesus, forgive us our trespasses, we beseech You.

You pray that your sins may be forgiven you in the same measure as you forgive those who trespass against you, without realising that if your sins were really forgiven as you forgive those of others, it would be a very miserable thing.

This is what your heavenly Father is telling you with these words.

AND LEAD US NOT INTO TEMPTATION

Lord, deliver us from hard trials.

Lord, we are weak.

Do not let our trials, O Lord, lead us to ruin.

BUT DELIVER US FROM EVIL

Lord, deliver us from evil.

May we succeed in finding something worth while in our trials, a step forward in our LIFE.

AMEN

So be it, Lord, Thy will be done.

THE ROSARY OF JESUS

The Rosary of Jesus is in remembrance of the 33 years of His Life. In Erzegovina this Rosary was often recited, especially during Lent. In the past, the Rosary contained a specific passage which was recited for each year of Jesus, before the Our Father. In recent times, the recitation of this Rosary has been limited to the 33 Our Father's, the Creed, plus a few additions.

During an apparition in 1983 to the visionary Jelena Vasilj, Our Lady gave not only the form but also suggestions as how to recite this Rosary:

1. HOW TO RECITE THE ROSARY OF JESUS

a) *contemplate the mysteries of the Life of Jesus* helped by a brief introduction. Our Lady urges us to pause in silence and to meditate on every single mystery. The mystery of the Life of Jesus must speak to our heart...

b) *It is necessary to express a special intention for each mystery*

c) After expressing the special intention, Our Lady recommends us to open our hearts together in spontaneous prayer during the contemplation

d) for each mystery, after the spontaneous prayer, choose *a suitable hymn*

e) after the hymn, *recite the five Our Father's* (except for the seventh mystery which finishes with three Our Father's)

f) after this we must *exclaim*: « O Jesus, be strength and protection for us! »

The Virgin Mary told the visionary not to add or take away anything from the mysteries of the Rosary. It must all remain as explained by Our Lady. The following is the complete text which has been given to us through the little visionary.

2. THE METHOD OF PRAYING THE ROSARY OF JESUS

THE CREED

1st Mystery:

* Let us contemplate « *the Birth of Jesus* ».
  We must speak about the birth of Jesus...
* Intention: let us pray for peace
* Spontaneous prayers
* Hymn
* 5 Our Father's
* Exclamation: « O Jesus, be strength and protection for us! »

2nd Mystery:

* Let us contemplate « *Jesus helped and gave all to the poor* »
* Intention: let us pray for the Holy Father and for the Bishops

3rd Mystery:

* Let us contemplate « *Jesus trusted in His Father completely and carried out His Will* »
* Intention: let us pray for priests and for all those who serve God in a particular way

4th Mystery:

* Let us contemplate « *Jesus knew He had to give up His Life for us and He did so without regrets because He loved us* »
* Intention: let us pray for families

254

5th Mystery:

* Let us contemplate « *Jesus made His Life into a sacrifice for us* »
* Intention : let us pray so that we, too, may be capable of offering our life for our neighbour

6th Mystery:

* Let us contemplate « *the victory of Jesus: He has overcome Satan. He is arisen* »
* Intention : let us pray that all sins may be eliminated so that Jesus may re-live in our hearts

7th Mystery:

* Let us contemplate « *The Ascension of Jesus to Heaven* »
* Intention : let us pray that the Will of God may triumph, so that His Will may be done.

After this, let us contemplate how « *Jesus sent us the Holy Spirit* »
* Intention : let us pray so that the Holy Spirit may descend upon us.

* 7 GLORY BE'S TO THE FATHER, TO THE SON AND TO THE HOLY SPIRIT.

Stabilimento Grafico Scotti S.p.A. - Milan
Printed in Italy - 1988